Don't Call Me Ma

Also by Sam Churchill

BIG SAM

Don't Call Me Ma

SAM CHURCHILL

DOUBLEDAY & COMPANY, INC.
GARDEN CITY, NEW YORK
1977

Library of Congress Cataloging in Publication Data
Churchill, Samuel, 1911-
Don't Call Me Ma.
1. Churchill, Samuel, 1911-
2. Lumbermen—Oregon—Biography.
3. Western Cooperage Company.
4. Clatsop Co., Or.—Biography.
I. Title. SD537.52.C49A3   634.9'82'0924 [B]
ISBN: 0-385-08481-1
Library of Congress Catalog Card Number 77-70895
Copyright © 1977 by Sam Churchill
All Rights Reserved
Printed in the United States of America
First Edition

To my wife,
Dorothy,
Who kept saying,
Write it

Contents

Maps precede page 1.

Don't Call Me Ma

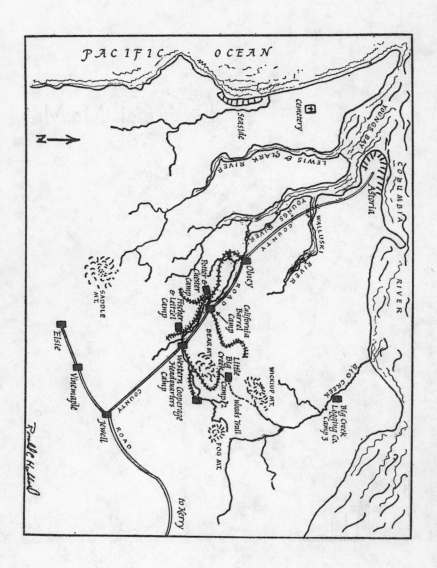

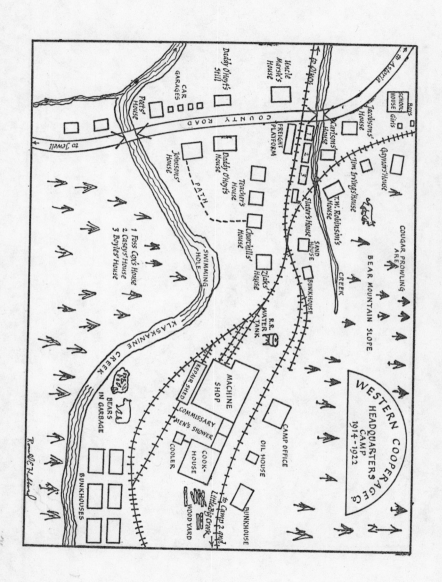

1
Bunker Hill and Paul Revere

Along with inspiring me to love God, trust nature, and be kind to animals, Mother insisted on good marks in school, a clean face and hands at the dinner table, and a proper respect for Boston.

Just why she insisted on ranking Boston right up with the Bible, green trees, and logging was as puzzling to me as a small boy as it was to the rest of the folks at the Western Cooperage Company's logging camp in northwest Oregon.

And as soon as I was old enough to talk instead of gurgle and could understand words, I could see that Boston was going to be a problem.

I knew she grew up there, met and married Dad there, and came West to Oregon and the Western Cooperage camp as a bride. But then you would have thought that with me coming along and her getting established in a new way of life in a remote Columbia River logging camp she wouldn't have had time to think about Boston. But she did.

I think it disturbed her that as I got near school age I was more interested in girls, big trees, and logging than I was in her yarns about Boston. I did gather, though, that in her eyes Boston was some sort of a Garden of Eden where all the good people were named Snow (her family name) except for a Mr. Paul

Revere who rode horses and a Mr. Benjamin Franklin who flew kites.

I learned later that Mr. Franklin didn't really become famous until after he moved to Philadelphia. But Mother said that didn't matter one iota. She said what did matter was that Mr. Franklin was born in Boston, went to school there, and learned the printing trade there. He didn't move to Philadelphia until he was seventeen years old, and that, said Mother, made him a Bostonian no matter what the history books and the good people of Philadelphia said.

Actually, I couldn't see that it made much difference one way or the other because by the time Big Sam Churchill came riding out of the big timber country of Oregon (by train) to Boston, Mr. Revere and his horse were dead and so was Mr. Franklin.

But the Snows had multiplied like polliwogs in a frog pond and were in walk-up apartments and houses all over Boston. Grandma Snow and Mother lived in a walk-up at 200 Princeton Street, in East Boston. Mother had two sisters, but they were married and gone by the time Dad arrived on the scene.

The Snows were a seafaring family: that is, all except Grandpa Snow. He liked the sea but every time he went on a ship he got seasick. He finally gave up trying to go to sea and settled down on dry land at Bucksport, Maine, where he bought a tannery. That was sort of disgusting to the rest of the Snows as well as to Grandma's folks, who were mostly sea captains.

Bucksport was where Mother and her two sisters were born. The tannery didn't seem to pan out, so Grandpa sold it and moved his brood to Boston, where he got a job as chief engineer on a Boston Harbor tugboat. Grandpa was happy on the tugboat and he didn't get seasick, but something worse happened. He died. The year was 1900 and Mother was twenty-one.

I never did get to see Grandpa Snow because he was dead and gone just like Mr. Franklin before Dad ever came to Boston. I never got to see Grandma, either, because she died just two years after I was born.

Come to think of it, I never did have any grandparents. I mean real, live ones such as you read about in storybooks. I mean where you can go on birthdays and Christmas and eat all the candy and other good things you want and no one ever says anything. Grandpa and Grandma Churchill died long before I was born. They are buried on a hill called Churchill Hill close to a place called Crouseville that Mother said is in Maine.

After Grandpa died Grandma Snow and her three daughters didn't have much so the girls had to go to work. Mother became a clerk at a place called C. F. Hovey's, a very fine stationery store where a lot of proper Bostonians came for calling cards, note paper, and stationery.

Hovey's was a quiet, genteel place where fingernails were always clean, hair combed, and shoes polished. And everyone spoke almost in whispers. Back in those days Mother wore funny hats and, in a long skirt with petticoat, blouse, and high-buttoned shoes, was just short of weighing one hundred pounds. The girls didn't have much money but Grandma saw to it that they went to stage plays and operas even if they had to climb stairways to the top balcony where the seats were the cheapest.

Dad, now, was a baked bean from a different pot. He was born on Grandpa Churchill's homestead on the banks of the Aroostook River near Crouseville, Maine. Grandpa raised spuds. Spuds took a lot of work and since Grandpa and Grandma didn't have much money they raised their own workers—nine boys and four girls. Dad was born in 1870 and he was just about in the middle of the thirteen kids.

Every spring big log drives came roaring down the Aroostook River and Dad and a younger brother, Marshall, were always on the bank watching and admiring the skills and happy-go-lucky life of the men who accompanied the drives. Dad and his brother didn't care much for spuds, cow dung, and milking but they did like logs and loggers. As soon as they were old enough to leave the farm they headed for the Maine woods. Eventually

3

they wound up in Oregon, Uncle Marshall in 1900 and Dad in 1902.

They came to Oregon to work for an uncle, and when they hired on he had two of the biggest, huskiest, most stubborn bone-and-muscle creatures you were likely to run across in the Oregon woods outside of the bull teams used to pull logs.

Dad worked hard in Oregon and prospered and so did Uncle Marshall. Dad liked Oregon but he was always hankering to go back to Maine for a visit, so about every other spring he would do that. On one of his trips he went to Boston to visit an older sister named Minna. That was her Bible name but everyone called her Minnie. Minnie and her husband had a grocery store right under Grandma Snow and Mother's apartment.

It so happened that Dad was his sister's favorite brother and Caroline Snow was her favorite friend. Without consulting Dad, she invited Caroline over for supper. Well, when Dad found out, beads of sweat began popping out of him from the top of his head to the ends of his big toes.

"Minnie," he protested, "I'm big enough and old enough to do my own pickin' and choosin'."

"You should be," agreed his sister, "but at forty years of age you haven't made much progress." Dad fussed, fretted, and fumed but he didn't make any progress that way, either. The year was 1910 and Mother was now thirty-one. But she was still trim, and easy with words, and held her head high as a good Bostonian should.

Dad had to admit to himself that he was glad she was there, sitting directly across from him at the table. Right in the middle of the blessing he tilted an eyebrow to take a peek at her and she was peeking at him. Dad told me later that Mother winked. Mother said she DID NOT. But it was of no account whether she did or didn't because by pumpkin pie and coffee time Dad was head over heels in love.

When Dad returned to Oregon he took a lock of Mother's hair with him. Mother's hair was as black as the inside of a coal mine when the lamps are out, and so fine you could run your hands through it and almost not feel it. Dad tucked it in an empty snuff (snoose, loggers called it) box and put it in his coat pocket next to his heart.

Grandma Snow had a conniption fit over that but she didn't say anything. Frankly, I think Grandma Snow had some uneasy moments about Dad. He was gentle and kind and big and knew a lot about Maine and Oregon and spuds and logging. But he didn't know much about history or Boston. Or the opera. And there was one other thing about him that was something of a problem—he didn't really chew snoose, or drink, or any of those things, but he did chew tobacco.

At the Western Cooperage camp, or any logging camp, be it Maine or Oregon, a fat chew of tobacco was the trademark of a good logger, the same as in Boston it was the trademark of a good baseball player. Grandma didn't like baseball, either. In Clatsop County, the county where the Western Cooperage camp was located, chewing was no problem. Dad and all the other men had a thousand square miles of canyons, rivers, primeval forests, and mountains in which to spit. In Boston it was different. Boston was full of cobblestones, concrete, and people. The only polite place to spit was from some wharf on Boston Harbor or behind a trash can in some alley. You couldn't do any of those with a lady like Mother along. So, when Dad was with Mother he didn't chew, and if it was a long evening he'd sometimes go almost crazy.

Anyway, before Dad returned to Oregon and the camp Mother talked him into getting engaged. At least, Dad, with a twinkle in his eye, said she did. Mother said she did no such thing. The way Dad told it, they were on the Boston subway one night when Mother shouted loud enough to be heard above the roar of the cars, "Sam Churchill, when are you going to ask me to marry you?"

Dad, being what you might call a man of few words, answered, "Now."

The day following the subway ride Dad bought Mother a diamond engagement ring. He showed it to Grandma Snow and she almost smiled. He slipped it on Mother's finger and she gave him a kiss. Dad then went back to Oregon with Mother's image firmly in place in his heart and the snoose box with a lock of her hair in his coat pocket.

Sometimes, I guess, he worried a bit about taking Mother away from Boston and into a way of life and an environment she had no way of knowing anything about or even imagining. Dad's sister Minnie said not to worry, that Caroline Snow was smart, strong-willed, and adaptable.

Early in March of the next year (1911) Dad returned and they were married. They honeymooned in Boston and Maine for three months before heading West to Oregon and what would be Mother's introduction to life in a remote and isolated lumber camp in the heart of Oregon's big timber country. It would be a breath-taking adventure for a woman who up until now thought that anything west of Waltham, where they made watches, was Indian country.

I don't know, but I think someday I might go to Boston. It might like me and I might like it.

I don't know for sure, but I think, maybe, I was conceived there.

2
Sky-high and Ten Feet Through

It was June 1911 and Mother was one of the first women to set up housekeeping in what the Western Cooperage liked to refer to as its "new and modern camp."

It may have been new but it was far from being modern, at least in terms of Mother's beloved old town of Boston. The nearest doctor was in the Columbia River town of Astoria, some twelve miles distant but a day's travel by logging train, foot, and motor launch. The stars and moon were her street lights. The logging railroad that divided the camp was the closest thing to a sidewalk.

And then there was Mrs. Johnson.

Mrs. Johnson, as Mother was soon to learn, was a proud, neighborly sort who lived in a tent house on the banks of Klaskanine Creek, who smoked a corncob pipe, and whose favorite expression when annoyed was "Bullshit."

I don't mean to imply that Mrs. Johnson was vulgar because she was not. She was a very capable, friendly neighbor who could deliver babies, castrate cats, and sometimes on Sundays give haircuts.

Another who soon got on Mother's doubtful list was Clarence (Daddy) O'Hoyt, a jolly, happy-go-lucky Irishman who lived with his wife, Ida, in a cedar shake house four houses down the railroad tracks from our house.

Daddy O'Hoyt's job with the Western Cooperage Company was supervising the boiler and big stationary steam engine that powered the company's machine shop. He was plump and had a walrus mustache and iron-gray hair.

Daddy O'Hoyt's job may have been overseeing the big, powerful stationary engine but his specialties were raising chickens and manufacturing moonshine whiskey. Oregon went dry in 1916 and Dad used to say that if it weren't for folks like Daddy and Ida O'Hoyt, half the loggers at the Western Cooperage would have withered like raisins in the hot sun and died of thirst. And all that in a land where seventy-five inches of rainfall a year wasn't unusual.

Actually, Daddy O'Hoyt despised chickens and wouldn't give the time of day to any kind of an egg, even one right out of the Easter Bunny. The only reason he put up with chickens was to get rid of the telltale mash and help hide the odor of the still he had going full blast in the loft of his henhouse.

One of the jokes going around the Western Cooperage camp was that the reason Daddy and Ida O'Hoyt's chickens made such fine stewing hens was that they were half stewed before they went into the pot.

Dad said the O'Hoyt hens were the only ones he knew of that would chortle and cluck all the way to the chopping block.

Mother said they were alcoholics.

But no matter what you said or thought, there was no denying that Daddy and Ida O'Hoyt's chickens were a bargain. After a few months of their egg laying and eating mash the O'Hoyts would sell them off for a dime apiece and bring in a new batch.

Mother and Dad rarely touched hard liquor and that used to amuse Daddy O'Hoyt. He said anyone who stewed one of his hens would be eating meat that was 90 proof.

There was one other person that Mother had reservations about. That was Mr. T. W. Robinson, the boss and the man re-

8

sponsible for the whole camp and its logging operations. It was he who decided where the camp would be located, who would live where. He was the one who settled disputes, arbitrated family arguments, set wage scales, and hired and fired.

And it was Mr. Robinson who decided the water supply for the camp would come from Klaskanine Creek, a frigid, fast-flowing mountain stream that bordered the camp area on the south. When it came time to pipe the water from the creek to the family houses and work areas Mr. Robinson kept things simple. There was no inside plumbing other than the family chamber pot under the bed for night use. The water lines were brought to each family's porch. There was no shutoff valve on our water pipe, so it gushed and burbled day and night.

Water from Klaskanine Creek came to us exactly as nature had made it. It was ideal for drinking, cooking, bathing, swimming, and fishing but it sometimes deposited unexpected bonus items in the Churchill water bucket. These included squirmy frogs, live trout, water dogs, and a variety of twigs and squishy water bugs.

The first frog to come to Mother's attention plopped headlong from the pipe into a pitcher Mother was filling with water for lemonade. Frogs were no novelty at the Western Cooperage camp. They laid eggs, thrived, and matured in dozens of ponds and backwaters from Klaskanine Creek. Their throaty chorus at night was a lullaby of sound that soothed weary fathers and mothers and drowsy youngsters to sleep.

But the little fellow who plopped into Mother's pitcher was in no mood for singing. He didn't take to the unfamiliar mixture of lemon juice, sugar, and water. At the sight of him trying mightily to climb the lip of the pitcher Mother let out a shriek and dropped the pitcher. It landed on a layer of small creek stones and gravel that Dad had spread under the pipe to reduce erosion and mud from the constantly falling water. The pitcher shattered into a zillion pieces, and when last seen the little frog was

9

scooting down the drain ditch that would lead him back to Klaskanine Creek and freedom.

"I wouldn't drink a dipper of our water in the dark if I were dying of thirst," Mother complained to Mr. T. W. Robinson, the camp superintendent.

Mr. Robinson was a product of those early days in logging camps when life in the big woods was simple, freewheeling, and male. The presence of Mother in the camp tended to make him very cautious and suspicious. He could see in her a trend that could doom decades of male domination in the timber country of the Far West.

"What's the matter with the water?" he asked a little brusquely.

"It has everything in it from frogs to polliwogs," answered Mother, letting a good measure of disgust show in her voice.

Mr. Robinson pulled a can of snoose from his shirt pocket and tucked a healthy chew under his lower lip, meanwhile trying to frame an answer to what to him must have been a stupid complaint.

Mr. Robinson was a very fine person and a good logger but he had an image to sustain. He was superintendent and it didn't please him one bit to listen to a complaint about his new camp, especially from a woman. It was he who had casually mentioned to Dad a week or so after Mother's arrival in camp that it was getting so a fellow had to duck behind a stump these days to urinate. He didn't say "urinate," but "urinate" was the word Dad used when telling the story to Mother.

Ignoring the implication of Mr. Robinson's remark, Dad suggested the company carpenters get busy and build some outhouses. He said no worker in the Western Cooperage Company camp should have to seek out a stump or bushes when nature called. Especially the camp superintendent. He invited Mr. Robinson to use the Churchill family outhouse, especially during periods of rain.

It was obvious that Dad was having a bit of fun at Mr. Robinson's expense, but Mr. Robinson gave no hint. Besides, there was merit in Dad's offer. The Churchills had the only outhouse in camp and the reason was that the camp was still under construction and the priority was for production structures such as a machine shop, office, bunkhouses, and a cookhouse before winter. Since Mr. Robinson hadn't planned on a woman in camp so soon there had been no pressure to build outhouses.

Dad dug the pit, split the shakes, and built a snug single-seater for him and Mother. It was fully equipped with a door and an outdated Montgomery Ward catalogue that for decades was a popular logging camp substitute for toilet paper.

But getting back to Mr. Robinson, the camp water, and Mother. Mr. Robinson mulled the complaint and his chew of snoose for a long moment. Finally, pushing his hat back a bit and hooking his thumbs in the loops of his suspenders, he gazed at Mother with momentary dislike.

"Caroline," he drawled at last with exaggerated constraint, like an exasperated teacher reprimanding a pupil, "frog legs are a delicacy. At the Western Cooperage we pipe them right to your door, for free. That's the same," he reminded her, "as you pay for your water and your house. So try them. Maybe you'll like them."

I don't think Mr. Robinson noticed but Mother's answering smile was a tiny streak that barely put a crinkle in the corners of her mouth.

"I will," she promised quietly, "I'll do exactly that. I most certainly will." And she did.

It was a month or so later that she invited Mr. Robinson over to our house for supper. During the several months she had now been in camp she had become a pretty good cook, specializing in hearty logger-type foods such as thick dark gravies with plenty of boiled or mashed potatoes and meat. But for Mr. Robinson she also had vegetables fresh from the Churchill garden, wild honey that Dad and a neighbor had gotten from a bee tree, hot biscuits, and for dessert a luscious wild blackberry pie made from berries picked by her own hand.

For Mr. Robinson there was also a special treat—a heaping platter of golden brown frogs' legs, deep-fried in a skillet of hot grease like doughnuts.

Dad stared at the heaped-up platter of legs with a look of total bewilderment.

"Caroline," he asked, "what in the devil are those?"

"Frogs' legs," said Mother, smiling.

"Frogs' legs!" Dad looked as though he might vomit. Mr. Robinson looked as though someone had dropped a handful of worms into his opened mouth.

"Frogs' legs," repeated Mother. "They are a delicacy. Mr. Robinson said so."

Being the camp superintendent, Mr. Robinson could have fired Dad on the spot and banned Mother from the Western Cooperage camp forever. But he did neither. He just sat staring at the platter of frogs' legs and swallowing. Finally, aiming a grim little smile at Mother, he picked up a serving fork and speared a plump portion of leg. Holding it poised above the platter, he studied it carefully, turning the fork as he pondered.

"Caroline," he finally asked with what appeared to be genuine interest, "are these damned things really good to eat?"

Mother seemed to be getting greener by the moment but she managed a nod of her head. "I'm taking your word for that," she added lamely, in what might have been an effort to shift all blame for whatever might happen to Mr. Robinson.

Mr. Robinson sat erect in his chair and, holding the fork with its load of leg at arm's length for all to see, squinched his chair closer to the table and announced, "If those fancy Easterners can eat 'em and like 'em, by God so can we." With that he shook the speared frog's leg onto Mother's plate.

"You've got to be joking," gasped Mother.

"Not on your life." Mr. Robinson grinned, and he speared a serving for Dad and one for himself.

Mother looked stunned. Dad swallowed and kept swallowing.

"There is real meat in the oven," Mother announced, her voice alarmed and her shoulders sagging in defeat.

Mr. Robinson was busy with knife and fork slicing off mouthfuls of frog meat. He stuffed a forkful into his mouth and turned to Mother.

"This is real meat," he said, chewing heartily. "Who wants plain old beef when he can have genuine Klaskanine Creek frogs cooked by a lady fresh from Boston?"

"These are not from Klaskanine Creek," snapped Mother, ruffled despite the haunting mental image of whole frogs breast-stroking around in Mr. Robinson's stomach. "These are commercial . . ." Her voice trailed off into silence as her tongue wrestled with the words "frogs" and "legs." She started over. "This was a special order," she said, "shipped from Portland to Astoria and then out here to me."

Mr. Robinson nodded and continued chewing with vigor and apparent relish.

"These things don't taste at all like frogs," he declared, looking at Mother and Dad. "Try them. They taste a lot like chicken."

Dad sat in his chair looking dazed, ill, and bewildered. Mother was the color of a live frog. Neither had made a move toward sampling a leg. Finally, Dad could stand it no longer. Pushing his chair back from the table, he stood up and grabbed the platter of frogs' legs and the serving from his and Mother's plates. Stepping outside, he heaved platter and all as far as he could heave them into the underbrush. Striding back inside the house, he sat down, nodded at Mother and the oven.

"Now," he announced, eying Mr. Robinson, who was still chewing a portion of frog leg, "we'll settle down to a supper of meat."

Mother dutifully retrieved from the oven a roast of beef. Dad sliced and served it. Mr. Robinson went to work on it with vigor spurred by hunger, and as far as I know that was the last time anyone ever served frogs' legs at the Western Cooperage camp.

From that time on, Mother seemed to get along first rate with Mr. Robinson, and when he brought his wife, Lucille, to the camp she and Mother became close friends. They quickly teamed up as a committee of two pestering Mr. Robinson for various improvements in living conditions in the camp. Among the first was the construction of several outhouses and screening of intakes to keep frogs and fish out of the pipes that transported water from Klaskanine Creek to the camp.

Another was the construction of a small shower room in the machine shop so the bachelor men would have a warm place to take a bath. The power machinery in the shop was run by belts and pulleys that got their power from a big stationary steam engine fed by a boiler, so there would be plenty of hot water for a shower.

Mr. Robinson didn't take to the idea at first.

"These men are loggers," he argued, "but you women want to treat them like babies."

Mother and Mrs. Robinson argued that they might be loggers but the important thing was that they were humans and deserved to be treated as such.

"You don't give them much choice," Mrs. Robinson said to her husband. "In time they either smell to high heaven or bathe in the creek and run the risk of being sterile for life."

The risk of sterility from bathing in the creek was a shocking revelation to Mother. "Why?" she wanted to know.

"Because," said Mrs. Robinson, "that water's so cold it could freeze a man's balls off."

The look on Mother's face put Mr. Robinson in such a good mood he ordered the shower room built.

The men of the Western Cooperage camp were molded for the times. Our northwest Oregon of 1911 was a rugged, topsy-turvy land of cascading streams and rivers, jammed with canyons, valleys, and mountainous peaks and ridges carpeted with trees. The Western Cooperage was in the heart of the Douglas fir belt, a massive, living, shimmering forest reaching from the crest of the Cascades to the sands of the Pacific Ocean and from Alaska into northern California.

"This is a land of God, trees, and muscle," Dad boasted to Mother on one of their Sunday afternoon walks. Walking was a popular family activity when the husbands weren't hunting, fishing, or cutting the winter wood supply. There were a few woods trails but most of the walking was confined to the logging railroad tracks. The railroad wound down the canyon alongside Klaskanine Creek. Walking seemed to strengthen one's ties with God and nature. In many areas the tracks cut through virgin lands where sky and tops of giant Douglas fir seemed to fuse, bridging the gap between heaven and earth. Mother never tired of those family Sunday walks and the spectacle of sky and earth and the insignificance of man. She used to impress upon me that at the Western Cooperage God and nature were our church.

Oregon's Douglas fir, named after pioneer botanist David Douglas, sent out from England to the Hudson's Bay Company's Fort Vancouver where Vancouver, Washington, now stands to do extensive research into the region's plant life, fascinated Mother.

"They are indeed fashioned by God to fit the immensity of Big Sam's land," she once wrote to Grandma Snow in Boston. And fit the land they did. Towering as much as three hundred feet in height and ranging from five to fifteen feet in diameter, they dominated the land and the people. It was the Douglas fir more than any other living thing that created our life of monster machines and a special breed of men like my father, Big Sam, armed with muscle, skill, and a driving urge to wrestle these rooted giants from the arms of nature.

I don't think Dad had been inside a church since his farm boy days in Maine but the sight of a towering Douglas fir straight and true as an arrow with nary a limb for maybe one hundred and fifty feet was like opening the Book of Genesis.

"You wonder how God could do all that in six days," he used to marvel.

But whereas Dad was enthralled and challenged by nature and the works of God and His might, Mother tended to be awed and a little fearful.

"Everything is so massive, so remote, so wild," she remarked to Dad one time while out among the big machines taking photographs with her Brownie camera. They were standing on the rim of a wooded canyon that could have accommodated Boston Harbor with room left over in which to tuck Bunker Hill and half of East Boston.

"Out here a man has air to breathe and room to move," Dad agreed. They watched a big steam donkey engine wrestle several tons of Douglas fir log through brush and timber from stump to landing. From their vantage point spurts of steam and smoke from a half-dozen other engines were visible, as were the jungles of stumps and trash left behind by crews of men and their marauding machines. Mother always referred to these as the "leftovers" of logging. The sight of torn trees, gouged land, lonely snags, and silent stumps sickened her.

"What will we do when all of the trees are gone?" she once asked Dad.

"That day will never come," declared Dad with firm confidence. "Caroline," he insisted with a note of impatience, "they's enough trees within the sight of our eyes to last forever."

My father believed that, as did a majority of the loggers of his day. Mother was never quite so certain.

3
Double or Nothing

Although Mother was the first woman to set up housekeeping in the Western Cooperage camp, other wives began arriving shortly. Among the first were Mrs. Guy Lillich, Mrs. Johnson, and Mrs. Kneeland. All three were Westerners by birth and loggers' wives by choice.

It was Mrs. Kneeland who quickly diagnosed Mother's bouts with morning sickness as having nothing to do with drinking water from Klaskanine Creek, hearty, calorie-laden logger-type meals, or a nervous stomach.

"Your problem is your husband," she told Mother; "you're pregnant."

"I can't be," gasped Mother. "We've only been married four months."

"You Easterners don't waste any time," agreed Mrs. Kneeland with a comforting little grin.

Mrs. Johnson, the first of the new arrivals to make a formal social call on Mother, concurred with Mrs. Kneeland's diagnosis.

She came strolling up the railroad track in her favorite day wear—baggy house dress, felt slippers, and a corncob pipe in her mouth. Mother was having a cup of tea, which was about the only thing that seemed to help settle her stomach. She poured

Mrs. Johnson one. Mrs. Johnson promptly poured a portion into her saucer and, blowing on it, explained that she never had been able to swallow hot liquids.

With both elbows on the table and after a careful scrutiny of Mother, she predicted that "in another five months you'll have a belly full of a Little Sam and before you can say Happy New Year they'll be diapers hanging on your clothesline."

She was right on all counts. I was born December 6, 1911, and my name was Sam. Two Sams under the same roof and in the same camp got to be a bit confusing. The camp people resolved the problem by referring to Dad and me as Big Sam and Little Sam. Mother referred to us as Sam and Samuel.

Mrs. Johnson was an enigma that Mother had a hard time living with and that the camp couldn't live without. Her English was atrocious, leaning heavily to "I seens" and "I ain'ts." For the most part it was strictly logger with a colorful array of cuss words that could curl the bark right off a Douglas fir stump.

"I don't ever want that woman in my house again," Mother fumed to Mrs. Lillich one day after one of Mrs. Johnson's visits. Mrs. Lillich was a gentle, friendly woman who, on her arrival at camp, had spent several weeks living in a tent while her husband was building the little one-room shack that would be their home. She had known Mrs. Johnson before and agreed that on occasion she could indeed raise hell with the king's English. Mrs. Lillich seemed always to find enough good traits in a person to balance off the bad.

"Sometimes," she admonished Mother, "a person's tongue can give a wrong impression." She said in the case of Mrs. Johnson, Mother should ignore her tongue and look at her heart.

Mrs. Johnson without a doubt could outcuss almost any logger in camp; she smoked a corncob pipe; she could drink Daddy O'Hoyt's chickenhouse booze straight out of the bottle without losing her voice or gasping for breath; and she could stun you with a blast of profanity and turn right around and stay by your bed all night if you were sick.

Mother could never quite bring herself to accept Mrs. Johnson completely but she did recognize in her a strength, courage, and compassion that were always there for others to draw on when tragedy struck or fear invaded the senses.

I remember Mother telling Dad one time that "she has the foulest mouth I have ever heard but deep inside, Sam, she is a woman of God and a Christian."

Dad's only comment was that although he didn't mind having her around on earth he didn't look forward to putting up with her in heaven.

Mother was to learn that Mrs. Johnson had other attributes and that among them were subtlety and craftiness. Most of the time they remained mute and harmless, unnoticed flaws in a colorful personality. But whenever C. A. (Sharkey) Bramble, company bookkeeper and supervisor of the company commissary, came on the scene they sped through every nerve and fiber of Mrs. Johnson's body, with bared fangs and straining at their leash.

"One of these days I'm going to nail that sonofabitch to his commissary door," she raged to Mother after buying some meat and accusing Mr. Bramble of weighing his thumb. "The Western Cooperage don't need no logs," she shouted at Dad; "they's making a fortune off that goddamn Sharkey Bramble's thumb."

Others in camp, including Mother, felt pretty much the same way. The camp was remote and the company commissary was there because it was a necessary service. Its stock of items was limited and consisted mostly of things like sugar, flour, coffee, some essential canned goods, some fresh fruits when in season, and a few other items to tide a household over in the event an embarrassed homemaker ran out. Quantity buying of food supplies was either at Mrs. Olson's general store at Olney or at Ross, Higgins and Company in Astoria. Ross, Higgins was the cheaper but Mrs. Olson's was the closer.

Meat was one commodity the commissary kept in good supply. Most of the camp people relied on Dave Tweedle, a Nehalem Valley rancher, for pork. Mr. Tweedle fed pigs at the camp on cookhouse slop and leftovers. The company used a lot of beef, so several halves were brought in every week by logging train. The train picked them up at the log dump after a trip from Astoria to there by boat. The boat that delivered the beef carcasses also delivered the cookhouse and commissary supplies.

Even though the camp was quite remote in its day, there wasn't much chance of starving. There were always meat and staples at the cookhouse and company commissary. But there was no ice or artificial refrigeration. Meat was hung on hooks in a screened cooler. Cougar and bear had the spot marked, as did numerous other predators, but they quickly learned that the cookhouse staff was a dead shot with a rifle, even in the middle of the night. They soon knew to keep their distance.

The night call of a frustrated cougar, the screech of a prowling wildcat, or the guttural snort of a lumbering black bear often jerked Mother upright in bed out of a sound sleep. They were terrifying moments, especially when one would remember that the Churchill outhouse was fifty feet from the house and hidden in dense underbrush. Every Western Cooperage family had a chamber pot under the bed, but the wives and children were constantly haunted by the specter of a dire emergency such as a loose bowel or dysentery.

On one of Mother's first trips to Mrs. Olson's general store at Olney she came home with an oversized family pot. It was enamel and with the lid cost sixty-five cents. Dad thought the price outrageous. Mother agreed.

Dad pointed out that we already had a chamber piece under the bed. Mother pointed out that under no circumstance would she even consider going out to the Churchill outhouse in the middle of the night. The new unit was a stand-by, a reserve chamber to ensure that Mother and Dad, and later I, would never have to face the uncertainties of crouching on a cold wood seat in the dark with only a thin layer of cedar shakes between us and the creatures of the night who Mother was certain ringed the camp with a circle of drooling fangs from sunset to dawn.

Dad hadn't the slightest uneasiness about Western Cooperage nights and the forest creatures that prowled the camp.

"Caroline," he used to argue, "there isn't one thing out there that would hurt you. A bear or a cougar is more scared of you than you are of them."

Mother was not convinced. Even as an infant I shared her fears of the night. Throughout our years in the camp Mother and I used the chamber pot at night and Dad fearlessly faced wind, snow, or rain for the disagreeable sprint to the outhouse.

One day on her way to the company commissary Mrs. Johnson stopped by the house and asked Mother to go along. The commissary was a small shelved room with a counter squeezed in between the cookhouse and blacksmith shop. Mr. Bramble was the only person with a key to it, so you had first to go to the company office and get Mr. Bramble to open the commissary. Mother said she needed a couple of items, so would go along. The commissary, cookhouse, and shop were a couple of hundred yards up the railroad track from our house.

As the two women were leaving the house Mrs. Johnson took a twenty-five-cent piece from her apron pocket and handed it to Mother.

"I got me a plan to fix that Sharkey Bramble," she announced. "When him and me gets to arguing and I ask you if you have a two-bit piece, you give me this one," she instructed.

Mother was curious but Mrs. Johnson would reveal nothing more.

"I want you to be just as surprised as he's going to be," she said, chuckling.

Mother waited out on the railroad track while Mrs. Johnson went up the wooden steps to the office and got Mr. Bramble. He wasn't in a retailing mood.

"I've got a desk load of work," he grumbled as he crossed the tracks to the commissary, "so let's make this fast."

Mother got her two or three items out of the way quickly and Mr. Bramble wrote them down in a company charge book. Mrs. Johnson's main purchase was a big slab of beef. Mr. Bramble put it on the scales and announced a price of several dollars.

"How much without your goddamn thumb?" she asked Mr. Bramble.

"If you don't want it I'll put it back," snapped Mr. Bramble, lifting the hunk of meat off the scales.

Mrs. Johnson averred that Mr. Bramble's name fitted him perfectly.

"You got the right name," she rasped. "You're a thorny son-ofabitch."

Mother was getting uneasy but Mrs. Johnson was as calm as a fat trout in nearby Klaskanine Creek.

"You bein' kind of a sporting man," Mrs. Johnson said to Mr. Bramble, "I'm going to make you a sporting proposition. We'll flip a coin, double or nothing. If you win I pay double for this meat, your thumb and all. If I win I get it for nothin'."

Mr. Bramble said it was a deal.

"Mrs. Churchill, you got a two-bit piece?" Mrs. Johnson asked, turning to Mother. Mother handed her the quarter Mrs. Johnson had given her earlier. Mrs. Johnson tossed it toward Mr. Bramble.

"You flip and I'll call," she ordered, adding that "I'm taking a hell of a chance just letting you do that."

Mr. Bramble was getting red-faced and grim-looking but he grabbed the coin in mid-air and flipped it. Mrs. Johnson called out "Tails" and when the coin landed on the counter that's what it was.

"I win," shouted Mrs. Johnson just as Mr. Bramble reached for the coin. Mrs. Johnson beat him to it.

"Keep your paws off Mrs. Churchill's money," she snapped, scooping up the quarter and handing it back to Mother. "You better hang on to this," she warned, "he's sneaky enough to lift it out of your pocket." Turning back to Mr. Bramble, she ordered him to wrap up the meat and give it to her, "and don't you dare put it down on my account in the company book."

Mr. Bramble wrapped the slab of beef in an old newspaper, pushed it across the counter to Mrs. Johnson, and, looking grim as death, declared the commissary closed and told Mrs. Johnson to "get the hell out."

On the way down the track Mother returned the quarter to Mrs. Johnson and congratulated her on her good luck.

"Luck nothing," said Mrs. Johnson. She then showed Mother the quarter again, turning it over. Both sides were tails.

"It's my boy Fen," explained Mrs. Johnson, "he filed down two quarters and put the tail sides together. He's a good boy, my Fen is. A lot smarter than me or the old man."

"Aside from being foul-mouthed, Mrs. Johnson is a cheat." Mother smiled while recounting the events of the day to Dad after work that evening.

Dad wasn't one to favor cheating another, even in what many camp people would have regarded as an honest cause.

"If Sharkey ever finds out what happened, Mrs. Johnson will pay plenty for that meat and it will serve her right," said Dad.

"I suppose God will have something to say to Mrs. Johnson," agreed Mother.

I don't know whether God ever got around to saying anything to Mrs. Johnson, but He put a bug in the ear of the Johnsons' dog, Prince.

Mrs. Johnson was getting the roast ready to go into the cook-stove oven when Mrs. Peets from across the county road called to her. She went outside to see what Mrs. Peets wanted and when she stepped out the door Prince sneaked in and grabbed the roast. Mrs. Johnson saw him but too late. He disappeared into the underbrush.

"That thievin' mongrel," screamed Mrs. Johnson, "he's worse

23

than Sharkey Bramble." She threatened to turn Prince into an "it" when she next got hold of him. But she didn't.

"You can't castrate character into a dog," she told Mother later. "But I'd sure like to try it on that bastard Sharkey Bramble." She smiled in high good humor, knowing she had outsmarted Mr. Bramble even though Prince won the roast.

4
Sounds in the Night

A screech owl is a flat-faced night creature, brownish in color, with tufted ears and about the size of a man's fist. It is a member of the owl family but has the lung power of an elephant.

I guess there aren't any screech owls in Boston; leastways, Mother had never heard of one until she came West to the Western Cooperage camp in 1911. If you had grown up with Dad and Mother as I did, it would be hard to see how such a little feathered thing could almost break up a marriage before it had hardly gotten started. But that is what happened during Mother's first night in the camp.

I will have to admit that the night call of a screech owl can get under your skin, especially if you don't know what it is that is making the racket. Now, in Mother's case she thought she knew and that is what caused all the trouble.

When night came to a 1911 Oregon lumber camp it was like being in a subway when the lights go out. A full moon could make it almost like daylight, and on a clear night with billions of stars lighting your way you could see to walk the railroad track. But in Oregon's high Coast Range, where rain clouds and fog often cloak the rich, green timbered hills, the moon and stars get locked out. During such times forest nights are black.

Mother's first night in camp was such a night. Black as an oil pit and with unknown ground creatures rustling through the underbrush that pushed in close on the bedroom side of the house. Mother lay with eyes closed but sleepless, listening to the strange sounds and the steady rhythm of Dad's breathing. She wanted to get up and check the door lock and close the window but a growing weight of uneasiness held her to the bed and cuddled close to Dad.

Suddenly there was a stirring on the roof followed by an undulating shriek sounding for all the world like "Help. Help." Mother shot bolt upright. The terrorizing call continued. Claw-like sounds on the tar-papered roof sent spasms of fear racing through her. Dad's rhythmic breathing proclaimed that he was at peace with the world. Mother shook him but to no avail. She pounded his back, pulled his hair, and screamed in his ear, but except for a few grunts and a poke in the jaw from an elbow the only indication that Dad was alive was his breathing.

Meanwhile the creature on the roof raised its own voice to match the shrill terror in Mother's. Fear swept aside any mastery Mother might have assembled for the situation. Grabbing Dad's feet, she swung his legs from under the covers and off the bed. "There's a cougar on the roof," she screamed. "Sam, there's a cougar on the roof." With Dad half out of bed in a leaning position, she leaped back under the covers and pushed. "There's a cougar on the roof," she kept shouting, her voice now muffled by the covers.

Dad came around slowly, his mind struggling to shut out the unfamiliar sounds of a woman in panic. He pushed himself into a sitting position on the edge of the bed, staring blearily into the darkness. Mother's shouts finally sliced through the curtain of sleep and he heard the word "Cougar."

The cougar, or mountain lion, was not a novelty around the Western Cooperage camp; nor were the black bear, bobcat, elk, deer, or coyote. Outside of the black bear, which often prowled the cookhouse area looking for scraps, none had ever ventured

26

within the confines of the camp. But there could always be a first time.

With this thought slowly taking form in his mind, Dad sat perfectly still, trying to pierce the darkness with his now alert eyes. They riveted on a shadowy movement in the corner of the room. Without a moment's hesitation Dad reached under the bed, grabbed the chamber pot, and with a roar that would have drowned out a pride of lions heaved the pot and then charged. There was a crash of glass and slivers of pain shot through the bare soles of Dad's feet. He let out a howl of misery. Mother let out a scream that would have frozen a grizzly bear in his tracks.

The ruckus in the Churchill house had awakened some of the men and T. W. Robinson. He was the first on the scene. He tried the door and it was unlocked, so he came on in. He stumbled around in the dark for a moment but long enough for Dad to clobber him with one of his five-pound fists. The blow landed in Mr. Robinson's stomach and the wind went out of him with a whooosh. He was doubled over and gasping for breath when Jim Irving, the woods boss, and another fellow pushed into the room with a lantern.

I guess it was quite a sight. The Churchill home at that time was a one-room affair about the size of a railroad boxcar. One end was curtained off to serve as a bedroom. The other end, which was the main entrance, was the kitchen. A round, pillar-type table for dining, plus Dad's big wooden rocking chair, plus several straight-backed chairs, took up the middle.

Mr. Irving said that when he entered the room with his lantern Mr. Robinson was bent double, clutching his belly and trying to get his breath. Dad, in a nightshirt that came almost to his ankles, was primed and cocked to throw another ham of a fist at poor Mr. Robinson. Mother was a ball of moans and sobs on the bed under the covers. For all she knew, Dad was dead and within moments she would feel the claws and fangs of the cougar. A smashed mirror on the wall across from the bed had showered the floor with broken glass, which accounted for Dad's howl of pain and cut feet.

When the lantern light revealed no sign of a cougar and Mr. Robinson doubled over in torment and agony, Dad went over to him to apologize and help him get some air. Mr. Irving prodded the ball of blankets that was Mother and told her she could poke her head out now that everything was all right. The third fellow sat down in Dad's big chair and started to laugh, but one look from Dad and Mr. Irving and he seemed content to rock and remain quiet.

It took a little coaxing by Mr. Irving to get Mother to peek out, and when she did she was furious to see Dad getting a dipper of water from the drinking water bucket for Mr. Robinson.

"I could have died under these covers and your whole concern would have been for him," she snapped, glaring angrily at Dad and Mr. Robinson.

"A full-growed cougar couldn't have clawed his way to you through that ball of covers," thundered Dad. "Now git out of bed and help me with T.W.; I think he's going to be sick."

He was, and that kind of upset Mother, too.

She put on a robe and slippers and began sweeping up glass and getting the bedroom back in order. The one fellow finally left and went back to his bunkhouse. Mr. Irving stayed around to help Mr. Robinson home. After his vomiting spell Mr. Robinson seemed to feel better. He sat in Dad's big chair, rocked a bit, and gingerly explored the tender portions of his stomach. Eventually he seemed to be breathing easier and his complexion was getting back some of its outdoor color.

"What in God's name was going on down here?" he asked, looking at Dad.

Dad was stumbling around with words when Mother cut in: "There was a cougar on the roof," she said with a shudder.

Mr. Robinson rocked and looked at Dad.

"A cougar?"

"Well," began Dad rather lamely, "Caroline thought it was a cougar but she gets excited. She's from Boston, you know."

"I know goddamn well where she's from." Mr. Robinson grimaced, lifting his eyes toward heaven as though telling the good Lord: SEE, THIS IS WHAT I HAVE BEEN TELLING YOU MIGHT HAPPEN WITH A WOMAN IN CAMP.

"I know she's from Boston," repeated Mr. Robinson. "Now, what about a cougar?"

"It might not have been a cougar," confessed Dad. "It could have been a—"

"He wouldn't know anything about it," interrupted Mother; "he was asleep." She then told Mr. Robinson about the screeching and scratching she had heard on the roof and how she couldn't get Dad awake and how when she finally did he threw the chamber pot at something and broke the mirror.

In answer to Mr. Robinson's question as to why he threw the pot, Dad said he thought he saw something move.

"And you thought it was a cougar?"

Dad said he didn't know what it was, but if it had been some night creature that had hopped in through the open window he had hoped to scare it back out the window. But when he heard the sound of breaking glass he realized the shadowy movement he had seen was probably his own dim reflection in the mirror. Then when Mr. Robinson came bursting through the door and began bumping into furniture, Dad said, he didn't know what to think, so he took a swing at the first thing he saw moving.

"How was I to know it was you?" he asked.

Mr. Robinson made a wry face at being reminded of his sore stomach and Dad's fist.

Dad and Mr. Robinson palavered and conjectured while Mr. Robinson rocked and Dad studied the blood spots on the bottom of his feet. All concerned finally decided whatever had panicked Mother wasn't a cougar or a bobcat—that is, all except Mother. She wasn't about to settle for anything but a cougar. Neither

Dad nor Mr. Robinson paid any attention to her and that didn't improve her mood any.

Finally Dad hazarded a guess that what had been on the roof was an owl. Maybe a screech owl.

"They can make a damn sight more noise than a cougar, especially when you hear one in the middle of the night and he is less than ten feet from your head," explained Dad in defense of Mother.

"A screech owl?" Mr. Robinson's voice rose from bass to soprano. "Jesus Christ, Sam, do you mean to tell me Caroline rousted me and half the camp out of bed just because of a goddamn little screech owl?"

"She didn't know it was a screech owl," protested Dad; "she thought it was a cougar."

"And if you take a lantern and go up on the roof you'll find claw marks," said Mother. "That was a cougar."

Dad didn't say anything but he gave Mother a look that told her to zipper her mouth. Mr. Robinson rocked and muttered something about women. He finally got up and announced he was going home and going to bed. He headed for the door and Mr. Irving followed with the lantern. As he was going out the door he mumbled something more about women and logging camps.

"What a hell of a combination," he said to no one in particular as he headed out the door and into the darkness.

The next evening when Dad came home from work Mother insisted he take the ladder and climb up on the roof.

"You mark my word, Sam Churchill. You'll find claw marks up there."

Dad finally did as she wanted. He was up there so long, Mother got nervous. She went outside and saw him sitting on the edge of the roof over the bedroom area with his legs dangling over the side.

"Are you all right?" she asked.

"I'm all right," said Dad.

"What did you find?" asked Mother.

"Just what I expected," said Dad.

"Claw marks," prompted Mother.

"Owl shit," said Dad.

Mother gasped in horror at the four-letter word. It was the second time in as many days she had heard Dad swear. That was more times than in the year and a half she had known him.

5
High on a Hill

Moving day in an Oregon lumber camp was nothing like Mother had ever seen or dreamed of in Boston.

When the time came to move a camp, to keep it within easy reach of the receding line of green timber, anything that was useful and mobile went—houses and bunkhouses, office, storage sheds, cookhouse, schoolhouse, and machine shop equipment. The machine shop was too big to be moved as a unit, so it was often dismantled and rebuilt at the new site. All structures in a typical logging camp of the period were mounted on log skids, with the exception of temporary structures or overly large ones such as a machine shop.

At moving time the houses and other buildings on skids could be pushed or pulled to a loading site and be skidded aboard railroad cars for the trip to the new camp site. If the company had a locomotive crane, which the Western Cooperage did, most houses could be lifted, skids and all, by the crane and set on the cars.

Bunkhouses for the bachelor men were often mounted on railroad cars permanently and parked on rail sidings. When a camp was moved, a couple of locomotives would hook onto a string of car-mounted bunkhouses and haul them to the new camp location. After they had been positioned at the new spot the family houses and other mobile structures would be loaded and transported.

Within days a relocated camp would be settled and working. In no time at all, weeds and underbrush would rush into the abandoned site and within a matter of months it would be lost to the eye.

When the Western Cooperage moved what Mother liked to call "our honeymoon camp," it even took along the Churchill outhouse. When Mother saw that sharing space on the railroad flatcar that was carrying our house, cookstove, furniture, groceries, and even Dad's handsome supply of split firewood, she had a Bostonian fit.

"That's the most ridiculous thing I ever heard of," she protested to Mr. Robinson, "carting that ugly, smelly thing right along on the same car with us."

"It wouldn't look so ugly or seem so smelly if it was you who would have to build a new one if we was to leave this one behind," Mr. Robinson answered, somewhat crisply. "Besides," he added, as though talking to himself, "Sam did a good job on this little feller. It's weather-tight, snug, and sturdy and he likes it. And I like it," he added with emphasis, "and by God you may as well like it, Caroline, because it's going with us and it is going on this car."

It was unlike Mother to remain quiet after a snippy retort like Mr. Robinson's but there was something in the tone of his voice that warned her to keep her mouth closed, and she did.

"I had the feeling," she told Dad, later, "that if I said one single word he would sit me on that outhouse seat, tie me there, and let me ride that way the ten miles to the new camp."

Dad, knowing T. W. Robinson and his moods, agreed that Mother had done exactly right.

It wasn't long after Mr. Robinson's and Mother's "understanding" that Mr. Casey and Mr. Cox coupled their locomotives onto the dozen or more railroad cars loaded with camp houses, supplies, and machinery and other machine shop equipment and began the slow, careful trip over the new railroad line to the new camp site. Mr. Cox's locomotive was in the lead and Mr. Casey's brought up the rear as a pusher. The locomotive arrangement was a safety precaution so that, in case of a derailment or car couplings parting, there would be no runaway with women and children and camp equipment at the mercy of a free-rolling car.

To most of the camp wives and children on the train this was virgin country. The year was 1914 and I was six months short of being three years of age. I was ready for my afternoon nap as Mr. Cox and Mr. Casey pulled the whistle cords of their respective locomotives and Mother and Dad's "honeymoon camp" began to move. Mother settled me in a pile of sun-warmed blankets and in moments, lulled by the rhythmic sound of car wheels crossing rail joints and by the gentle sway of the train, I was sound asleep.

There was nothing in Mother's Boston, or in all of New England, that could have prepared her for this immense, virgin, and wild region. Except for the cleared route of the railroad, no timber had been cut. Mammoth Douglas fir ten feet or more in diameter crowded close to the tracks and marched, thick as hair on a dog's back, up, down, and over this jumbled land of fog-draped peaks, slopes, and what from a railroad car sometimes appeared to be bottomless canyons. These mighty firs, along with towering hemlock, spruce, and cedar, were a storehouse of replenishable wealth that would ultimately dwarf the frantic returns of California and Alaska gold, Nevada silver, and Montana copper.

Besides dwarfing nature's vast underground vaults of precious minerals, they dwarfed man's ability to compare, describe, or comprehend.

Mother, recalling her emotions in later years, used such terms as "exalted" and "celestial."

"From that railroad car, shared with that awful outhouse," she once told me, "I saw God in His glory, nature elated." I doubt that any of the other camp wives on that railroad car shared Mother's feelings. I know Mrs. Johnson didn't.

She remarked when the long train arrived at the new camp site that the jolting of the cars "damn near shook my guts out."

Cuddled in my blanket bed, I didn't feel any of the jolting that Mrs. Johnson mentioned. I slept mile after mile. Mother finally lifted me from the blankets and, holding me gently against her breast, sat silent, awed, and reverent while "God in His glory," with ever-changing scenes, seemed to keep pace with the slowly moving train as its two locomotives, sending up thunderheads of black smoke, crawled upward along the moderate but steady grade to the Western Cooperage Company's new headquarters camp.

This camp would be permanent and the nerve center of the company's expanded logging operations. It was here that my father would work for more than a quarter of a century. And it was here that he would die with the smell of the big woods in his nostrils, and the feel of calk shoes on his feet.

When the train arrived at the new camp Mr. Alex Carlson was waiting and ready with his locomotive crane. Some of the car-mounted bunkhouses had been brought up the previous day and were installed on a special storage track built for that purpose up near where the machine shop and office were located. Mr. Bramble was already doing his book work at the new location. The company commissary hadn't yet been brought up and that added to his pleasure.

Mr. Robinson and Mr. Irving had drawn up a camp plan. Mr. Robinson showed it to Mother and she was aghast. Mr. Robinson was not, by any stretch of the imagination, anything resembling a professional planner. His camp plan was a rough pencil drawing on a piece of tablet paper. Little drawn squares represented family houses on each side of a pencil line that Mr. Robinson told Mother was the railroad track. The biggest square was for the machine shop, which hadn't been rebuilt yet. Me-

35

dium squares indicated the cookhouse and office. One of the squares was labelled "Churchill," and Mr. Robinson told Mother that was our house. Mother didn't like the location. She wanted to be on the same side of the tracks as the schoolhouse. Mr. Robinson said that was no problem and proceeded to erase our name from the one square and put it on a square on the opposite side of the pencil line that was the railroad track.

Mr. Robinson looked up from his paper work with a smile. "Anything else?" he asked.

With his pencil-plotted paper in hand Mr. Robinson began supervising the unloading of the newly arrived family houses. Mr. Casey moved his locomotive onto a nearby siding and Mr. Carlson moved his locomotive crane into its vacated place. It was called a locomotive crane because it could move itself along the railroad tracks.

Within minutes cable slings were slipped under the ends of the log skids and the crane lifted Mrs. Lillich's house like a piece of ship's cargo from a dock, and deposited it a dozen yards or so from the tracks on the spot indicated by one of Mr. Robinson's squares. The tiny combined schoolroom and teacher's house was on the same car and it was lifted off and set on its spot. The housing spots were rough and still supporting a growth of underbrush. That didn't seem to bother Mr. Carlson or the crane crew. Mr. Carlson would set a house right down in the middle of the brush and slack off his crane line. If the house looked fairly level, that was it. The men removed the cable slings and moved on to the next house. The occupant was expected to do his own fine leveling with the aid of a borrowed company log jack. He could also make his own yard by clearing his own brush.

By the time Dad got in from work that night our house was in place, the crane crew had set up the cookstove, and supper was ready.

In little more than a week the machine shop had been dismantled at the old camp and the timbers moved to the new camp, where it was rebuilt and the machinery installed. In no time at all the new headquarters camp was a throbbing, pulsating community with houses on both sides of the railroad track and Klaskanine Creek, along the county road, and a hundred feet or so up the slope of Bear Mountain where Mr. and Mrs. Robinson, Jim Irving, and Mr. and Mrs. Mike Gaynor lived.

Mrs. Gaynor liked to say she lived high on a hill and Mother had to admit to being envious because from the Gaynors', or the Robinsons', a body could look right out over the entire camp, even to Mrs. Johnson's alongside Klaskanine Creek.

Even with more than two dozen families now living in the camp there wasn't that much to see outside of ripped trees, teetering snags, and dour-looking stumps.

But it was here that I would grow into boyhood and learn to trust God, love nature, and someday be a logger. Following in your father's footsteps was pretty much of a dream for every logger's son, but it created problems around our house. I was to learn that Dad and Mother had other ideas.

"I'm a logger because that is all I can do," Dad used to tell me over and over. He said he was a logger because he lacked an education. Working at the far end of a main-line cable hooking on logs for the big steam donkey engines to pull in might look exciting, Dad admitted, but it wasn't. "You work in mud, rain, and cold in winter and you sweat to death and choke in your own dust in summer," he used to stress in an attempt to discourage me from wanting to follow his footsteps into a career as a logger.

Mother and Dad never downgraded Dad's occupation and my desire to imitate him. Instead they aimed their efforts at interesting me in other careers and in getting an education.

"With an education you have a choice of careers," Mother would mention, almost casually, time after time during walks and reading times; "without an education your choice is limited." To Mother and Dad success and happiness were the rewards of those who set goals for themselves.

"Someday you will climb Saddle Mountain and from its summit you will look out over all of Clatsop County," Mother assured me, "but only if you really want to and plan to," said Mother. "That," she said, "is having a goal."

Saddle Mountain was Clatsop County's highest peak, a rugged, basalt upthrust that in eons past wrenched itself free of its Lewis and Clark and Youngs river basins and ended up towering 3,300 feet above its old environs.

Mother said that was one of the marvels of America: every young boy could be a Saddle Mountain. All he had to do was want to.

As I grew older I better understood what Mother and Dad were driving at but Dad began to emerge more as a man content to be high on a hill rather than one striving to attain some beckoning summit.

Dad had come West in 1902 to see his brother Marshall, who had deserted the pine and spruce country of Maine two years previously.

"They's a job out here for you if you come," Uncle Marshall had written Dad, who at the time was working in a Maine lumber camp.

Uncle Marshall worked for his Uncle Abe Crouse, an old Maine logger who was Grandma Churchill's brother. Uncle Abe came West in 1891 to see if the Oregon trees were as big as he had heard they were. They were even bigger, so he stayed. He started a little logging operation on Milton Creek near the small Columbia River community of St. Helens. By the time his nephew Big Sam Churchill arrived he had phased out his bull teams and horses and switched to a steam-powered donkey engine.

Trees were felled and bucked (sawed) into lengths the little steam donkey could handle. The donkey dragged them to the banks of Milton Creek. A dam, referred to as a splash dam, built of logs and timbers, held back the waters of Milton Creek until the store of logs along the banks was worth transporting to a mill. The gates of the splash dam were then opened and the rush of water swept the logs down Milton Creek some three or four miles to the Columbia River. Here they could be rafted and towed to a sawmill.

The method was crude but in those days most of the land adjoining Milton Creek was open. There were no environmentalists to protest and no laws to say he couldn't use the creek. So he did, and the result was that my father and my uncle and a couple of dozen other men had jobs.

Even then, at age thirty-two, Dad was big, powerful, and quiet. Uncle Marshall, nine years younger, was big, powerful, and brash. When the two men were together Uncle Marshall was the leader, Dad the follower. Uncle Marshall was a driver; a man determined. For years Mother tried to remake Dad, to lift his eyes to the summit where she was convinced he should be. Dad would protest.

"Don't push me, Caroline," he used to argue; "I am what I am." What Dad was, was a rigging man, one of the most dangerous jobs in the woods. Rigging men hooked the heavy cables to the logs so that the donkey engines could drag them in. Their workdays were an endless cacophony of screeching donkey whistles, jostling metal, humming steel cables, tumbling logs, and shouting voices. Dad's was a world of brute strength and catlike agility where the unwary, be it tree, man, or brush, ended up toppled, maimed, or shredded.

That was why Dad and Mother had a horror of my working in the camps. Mr. Jack Smith, the company's general manager whose office was at the company headquarters in Portland, gave them hope.

At the end of World War I, when Mr. Robinson left and a new superintendent was needed, Dad was the choice. He turned the job down.

"They want you to be superintendent, the biggest, most important job in the camp," Mother protested. "You owe it to the company," she argued. "You owe it to Samuel, to me. You owe it to yourself."

Dad stared at me sitting on my cot. He looked at Mother and then at Mr. Smith, who had come down from Portland to make a personal appeal. He took a chew of tobacco, then scratched his head. He stepped outside and I could hear him spit. He put his hands in his pockets. He took them out. He looked at Mother as though pleading for help. She smiled but said nothing. He looked at me and then back to Mr. Smith.

He shook his head and for the final time said, "No."

Shaking her head in disappointment, Mother got up from her chair and arranged three cups and saucers and a plate of big, fat sugar cookies on the table. She took the bubbling coffeepot from the wood stove and filled the cups.

I had a feeling she was almost in tears but she gave no real indication. Instead she smiled, took Dad's hand, and walked with him toward the table. She looked over her shoulder toward Mr. Smith and me.

"We may as well have some cookies and coffee," she said to Mr. Smith. "When Sam makes up his mind, it is better to eat than argue." There was a cup of hot cocoa for me.

Mr. Smith had to make one more try.

"Why?" he asked Dad.

"Because I only went to the third grade and I can barely read and write," answered Dad.

"Dammit, Sam," sighed Mr. Smith, "we don't want you to read and write. We want you to get out logs. We can hire accountants and retired schoolteachers to do the reading and writing. All we want you to do is log."

"Marsh could do it," suggested Dad.

"We don't want Marsh," persisted Mr. Smith. "We want you, Sam. Goddammit, you."

Dad reached for a fat cookie and a cup of coffee. Mr. Smith had been standing. He now sat down on the cot beside me and put a big hand on my shoulder.

"Samuel," he said, "you do what your mother and father tell you and when you get that college education you come and see me. If you turn out to be half the man your father is, I'll still want a Sam Churchill as superintendent of this Western Cooperage camp."

I wasn't quite sure whether I wanted to be a superintendent or not, but I smiled and said, "Yes, sir."

6

The King's English

Mother soon learned that loggers were as inventive with words and phrases as they were with tools and machinery.

A hooker didn't have to be a prostitute and Molly Hogan was no lady. A filer wasn't an office worker and butt rigging wasn't what she first thought. A schoolmarm wasn't necessarily a teacher and belly pads weren't something you wore next to your flesh over your belly.

To Dad they were everyday logger terms as common and as meaningful to a worker in the woods as "debit" and "credit" would be to a bookkeeper in an office.

A schoolmarm, Mother learned, was a tree that started out with a single stem, then branched out into a double.

"Like a man standing on his head with his legs spread out," explained Dad.

"Then why don't they refer to it as a schoolman?" challenged Mother.

Dad said he didn't know and he could care less. Besides, he added, no logger worth his salt would walk five feet to watch another logger standing on his head. But now, a schoolmarm, that would be different. Mother said he was disgusting. Dad said he couldn't help it if God made him a man and put man thoughts in his head.

In the cookhouse "armored tit" meant canned milk.

"Why do they insist on associating those vulgar names with women?" Mother asked my Aunt Blanche, a former schoolteacher who had married Uncle Marshall and lived down by the crossing.

Aunt Blanche pointed out that every occupation had its own peculiar pet names and that some of them weren't meant for mixed company. Electricians, for example, referred to male and female plugs "and if you can't figure that one out you do need help," said Aunt Blanche. It wasn't quite that obvious to Mother but she did finally figure it out.

"It still isn't as gross as 'armored tit,'" she insisted.

Aunt Blanche's maiden name was Blanche Murphy and she was teaching school at Masten Brothers camp up near St. Helens when she met Uncle Marsh. In later years she taught in a Portland business college. When I was having a terrible time with fourth grade fractions she tutored me, and if it hadn't been for her I think maybe I might have still been in the fourth grade, bogged down by fractions.

Aunt Blanche was far from being an authority on loggers' terminology but, although she was more of a bride than Mother, she had taught school in logging camps, so was a little more familiar with woods words.

When Mother asked about a woman named Molly Hogan that she had heard Dad mention, Aunt Blanche doubled over with laughter. Molly Hogan wasn't a woman. It was a short length of cable strand that a logger could quickly fashion into a wire loop by wrapping it back on itself. It was used as a temporary link to hook any number of things together, such as the eye ends of two cables. It was often used to replace a lost cotter key or as a guide for a whistle wire. A whistle wire was similar in size and shape to a stranded wire used for clotheslines. It ran from the steam whistle on a donkey engine's boiler out through the brush to where the unseen rigging crew hooked the logs to the big main-line cable. The signalman, called a whistle punk because in the early days he was often a young boy, was within sight or hearing of the rigging crew. By jerking the whistle wire he would blow the whistle. The whistle signals directed the donkey engineer.

When Mrs. Guy Lillich once casually mentioned that Dad had been a chaser Mother was stunned. Aunt Blanche had another good laugh but this time she was a little upset with Mother for having so little faith in Dad. A chaser, in logging terminology, she explained, was a worker who followed the logs in from felling areas. The big machines with their heavy drums of steel cables reeled the logs in, like a fisherman reeling in a fish. In the old ground logging days the logs came plowing in flat on the ground. They often hung up on roots or stumps. The job of a chaser was to free them. Chasing was a miserable job and about as dangerous as chewing on a dynamite cap, since the chaser was often within reach of moving lines, the deadly whip of a vine maple limb, and the crushing weight of a toppled tree or snag.

Mother was also uneasy about the term "hooker," which was short for "hook tender," the boss of a logging unit, or "side." She also learned that a logging camp filer had nothing to do with office routine. A filer was the skilled artisan who sharpened the teeth of the crosscut saws used by fallers and buckers. Saws used by timber fallers were narrow and up to ten feet in length. Those used by buckers (the men who sawed the felled trees into logs of varying lengths) were wider and usually not quite as long. Buckers and fallers were usually paid on a piecework basis, so a saw with teeth like a razor made their job easier and faster.

The only camp term Mother accepted readily was "Irish apples," sometimes used for potatoes.

"Utterly absurd," sniffed Mother, "but at least it is clean."

Two terms she couldn't bring herself to say were "bastard fir" and "butt rigging." A bastard fir was nothing more than a young

Douglas fir in the transition period from young mature, or red, fir into old mature, or yellow, fir. Dad described the process as similar to a man's aging from his late twenties into his early thirties.

"Butt rigging," she felt, was downright crude. All it was, was a length of heavy swivels and clevises connecting a donkey engine's main line (the heavy pulling line) to the haulback line. The chokers that formed a looped cinch around one end of a log were attached to the butt rigging. When the main line of a donkey engine was reeled in, the log or logs came with it. With the log at the landing and the choker unhooked, the haulback line was reeled in and pulled the butt rigging, chokers, and main line back out to the woods. Before the haulback line came into being the main line had to be pulled back out by manpower. Later some smart logging boss turned the job over to a horse, which he called a line horse.

Butt rigging also performed the same service as a swivel on the end of a fishing line—it kept the line from twisting. No matter what its use and its value, Mother disliked the term and would never use it.

The misunderstandings that arose from terms and expressions weren't all centered around logging. Mother had some strange expressions and terms that at times left the camp people wondering. Mother had the Boston habit of dropping and adding r's. An idea became an "idear." A bear became something that sounded like "ba." A calf became a "cough."

"If what you talk is the king's English, then I'm glad we got rid of the sonofabitch," Mrs. Johnson once told her. Mother prided herself on her use of proper English and she was tireless in her effort to see that Dad and I were as careful of the spoken word as she. My days of play were spent with youngsters who by the age of six were old pros in the use of "ain't," "seens," and total mix-ups in the use of "was" and "were." They also excelled in damns, hells, farts, pisses, sonofabitches, bastards, and other expletives of special value for special occasions.

Despite my daily encounters with the common-variety cuss words and poor English, Mother did succeed in making progress with me. One of her tools was books and magazines. An excellent reader, she read book after book and story after story to me. Sometimes it seemed she monitored every word in my mind as well as those that were spoken. At times it was almost impossible to communicate because of her corrections. But I did learn and a fair amount of good English has remained with me through the ensuing years.

Whatever glow Mother got from her success with me she lost when it came to Dad. In her words, he was "utterly incorrigible." A third grade education followed by years in Maine and West Coast logging camps gave Dad a speaking knowledge of English without any frills. He accepted "seens," "ain'ts," and all the other faux pas of grammar at their face value and used them with agility and innocence.

"There is no such word as 'ain't,'" Mother used to correct him.

"Then how come you just said it?" Dad would reply.

"You don't have to be so stubborn," Mother would say.

"I ain't stubborn," Dad would grunt.

Aunt Blanche used to come to Dad's rescue.

"If Sam wants to say 'ain't' let him say 'ain't,'" she used to argue with Mother. "What's it matter?"

"It matters because he is a wonderful man, a fine husband and a good father as well as a competent logger," Mother used to argue back. "Sam is a talented man. Poor grammar detracts from that talent."

Grammar, good manners, and education were important to Mother but she had one other obsession. That was what title to use when addressing her. The common term for a mother around camp was "Ma." A few kids, usually the older ones and only in private, would sometimes use "the old man" or "the old lady." I had an immediate dislike for those. I didn't like the implication of disrespect.

46

From as far back as I could remember I had addressed Mother as "Mother." It seemed to come naturally. She had a horror of "Mom" or "Mommy" as being unmanly for a boy. But "Ma" sounded both respectful and a little more grown-up than "Mother."

So one day I tried out "Ma." Mother's reaction was instant and final.

"Don't you ever call me Ma," she almost shrilled. "Calves call their mothers Ma," she added, stretching "Ma" into a long *Maaaaaa*. "I am no cow," she ended in what sounded like a huff. Aside from scaring all words out of me for a good five minutes, she convinced me. From that moment until her death in 1950 I called her Mother.

I guess I responded to some degree to Mother's dedication to education. She seemed encouraged and gratified at my progress in school and one day I overheard her tell Dad that "there is no reason Samuel can't study to be an engineer."

I could hardly believe my ears. Being an engineer was what I dreamed of. "Mr. Casey can teach me," I shouted. Mr. Casey was a locomotive engineer. He had a wife named Rose whom Mother liked, and a daughter named Mae who was a few years older than I was.

The Western Cooperage at that time had three locomotives, all a special logging breed of geared engine called a Shay. It was patented by Ephraim Shay, a Michigan logger, back in the 1870s and was an immediate success because it could follow a logger over most any kind of track and up and down grades of 10 per cent and more.

There were other types of locomotives developed for the logging industry and designed to operate on rough track in steep, rugged country. These were the Heisler and the Climax, also geared engines of comparatively light weight, compared with the big main-line rod engines that haul passengers and freight, but extremely powerful and versatile for their size. The Shay was the most popular and by 1945, when the Lima Locomotive

Works produced its last Shay, more than 2,700 had been built, mostly for the western logging industry.

Railroading had become big business in logging. The logging railroad was the link between the receding forest line and tidewater log dump or mill. By 1917 Oregon had some 600 miles of logging railroad and Washington State over 1,800 miles. Big rod engines handled the logging railroad's main-line chores and could handle from thirty-five to a hundred loaded log cars, depending upon whether or not there was any adverse grade. Spur lines reached out from the main line into the timber where the actual logging operations were. The small but powerful geared engines such as the Shay serviced these spur lines, bringing empty log cars to the landings (loading areas) and exchanging them for loaded cars, which they deposited on main-line sidings. Loaded cars from several logging units were gathered into trains and hauled to the log dump by the big main-line engines.

In its peak year of 1930 the logging railroad blanketed the wild, tumbled, timbered areas of the West with 7,200 miles of main-line and spur-line track. These big railroad outfits ranged from Weyerhaeuser Timber Company at Longview, Washington, with 170 miles of railroad to tiny outfits such as Fischer and Leitzel near our camp. Fischer and Leitzel had one weary but sprightly locomotive, a Climax, and some two or three miles of track.

Weyerhaeuser's Longview division had the largest locomotive ever built specifically for a timber company. It was a giant Baldwin 2-8-8-2 weighing 178 tons and it could drag one hundred loaded log cars up a 3.7 per cent grade. Polson Logging Company out of Hoquiam on the Olympic Peninsula in Washington State had 150 miles of railroad and thirteen locomotives.

Uncle Marshall once worked there.

"It's the damndest outfit I ever seen," he told us one night when he and Aunt Blanche were visiting Mother and Dad. One of the most exciting evenings a logging camp youth could hope for was a visit from another logger and his wife. During such visits the logging stories flowed with language and tales rich enough to keep a young boy's heart pumping with excitement long after the company had gone and he was tucked in bed for the night.

"Sam, they got so many goddamn locies [logger term for locomotives] over there a feller don't dare sit on a rail for fear one will come along and nip off a piece of his ass," was how Uncle Marsh described life at Polson Logging Company to Dad.

Aunt Blanche would interrupt the best stories ever with a stern "Marshall!" Uncle Marsh didn't swear as much as a lot of loggers but sometimes when he got excited about something he would forget and open up.

Dad rarely swore but when he did it was from something aggravating like bumping his head and you could hear him all over camp.

One of the most exciting railroad logging firms in the whole world was the Kerry Line in Columbia County, right next to our county, which was Clatsop. The Kerry Line had everything, including a tunnel that pierced a hump of the Coast Range and allowed its railroad to go from the Columbia River fifty or more miles into the Nehalem Valley with its rich stands of virgin timber.

From some of the higher ridges around our camp we could sometimes hear the whistles of Kerry Line locomotives, especially if the wind was right. The Kerry Line hauled not only its own logs but logs from a dozen or so outfits that paid Mr. A. S. Kerry, founder of the Kerry Line, to haul their logs over his main line. During busy seasons Kerry Line locomotives never stopped. They ran day and night with one crew relieving another when its work time was up. One time I got to ride with Frank Tate, a Western Cooperage locomotive fireman, who wanted to visit a cousin who had the same kind of a job at the Kerry Line's Camp Neverstill. There never was or will be a railroad logging camp quite like Neverstill. Log trains and the big machine shop operated day and night. It even had a hospital and in 1916 was officially noted as Neverstill Post Office.

When Mr. Kerry first established Camp Neverstill it was at the remote end of his rail line with the only roads into the area as bad as or worse than those to the Western Cooperage camp. Kerry log trains brought in loaded boxcars of supplies along with the strings of empty log cars. The supplies were for farmers in the area and for the many camps whose rail lines tied in with the Kerry Line. The Kerry Line logging road, officially known as the Columbia & Nehalem River Railroad, was a common carrier, so the company provided a gasoline-powered rail car for passenger service.

Mr. Kerry was a great sportsman with a particular interest in golf and baseball. The Kerry Line and many of its camps supported baseball teams, and on Sundays, before a game, the Kerry Line gasoline-engined rail cars would cruise the length of the rail network picking up fans and players and transporting them to the major games.

From the time it officially opened its railroad in 1915 to the end of its logging career in 1938 the Kerry Line hauled a staggering 3 billion 100 million board feet of logs. In terms of loaded cars that would be a log train stretching from Boston to Portland, Oregon.

You can see how railroading could get into the soul of any logging camp boy living in the steam era. If you couldn't be a locomotive engineer there were the big steam donkey engines that dragged the logs from the felling area to railroad spurs where they were loaded on cars.

These big, powerful machines were mounted on heavy log sleds to enable them to pull themselves from area to area as the line of timber fell farther and farther back. Mounted on its hewn log sled and with its reel-like drums carrying several tons of steel cables, a big Humboldt yarder such as the Western Cooperage used could weigh as much as two hundred tons. Clawing ever forward, like a thirst-crazed man seeking water, the steam donkey engine sought out every ridge top, creek, gulley, or canyon that had timber. They were big and they were deadly—deadly to man and nature.

And then there were the car-mounted skidders, giants of destruction that could clear forty acres of timber at one sitting. These behemoths of steam, steel, and greed weighed up to three hundred tons and it usually took two locomotives to move one. Their three separate engines, fed by one huge boiler, operated as many as twelve separate cable drums. A skidder dragged in and then loaded its own logs. The three engineers on a skidder were known as levermen.

But for me, being in the cab of a steam locomotive was the most exciting. The Western Cooperage's Shay No. 2, run by Mr. Casey, was just my age. It was delivered, brand new, to the company on Valentine's Day in 1912, just two months after I arrived.

If it is possible for a small boy of six and a machine to fall in love, little No. 2 (Two-Spot was its designation by the camp people) and I had an affair going. Most little boys learned about steam locomotives from kiddie books. I had a real live locomotive to love.

Mother's pronouncement that I was a likely prospect to become an engineer was the answer to all my dreams.

"Mr. Casey can show me how to run No. 2, then when he gets old I can be her engineer," I told Mother.

Mother sat me in my little rocking chair and then sat herself on the linoleum floor in front of me. I could look directly into her eyes and they seemed sad and troubled. She took both of my hands in hers.

"Mr. Casey would like that." She smiled at me. "I just know he would." Spotting an untied shoelace on one of my shoes, she busied herself with that for a moment and then continued, "But wouldn't you rather be the friend who planned the railroad lines for little engines like No. 2? A nice railroad that would be solid and not too steep would make the work of little engines like No. 2 a lot easier. Just think how happy and proud No. 2 would be to haul logs on a railroad that you built."

I shook my head. I didn't want to build track. I wanted to sit in the cab across from fireman Oscar Ward just like Mr. Casey and feel No. 2 strain and quiver when I pulled the throttle and gave her the steam. I wanted to hear the rolling thunder of flaming oil in the firebox. I wanted to thrill at the thunder of the exhaust blast from her stack.

"I want to be the engineer of No. 2 just like Mr. Casey," I insisted.

Mother nodded, got to her feet, and tousled my hair. "We'll ask Mr. Casey and see what he says," she said, smiling.

The next morning Mother and I were up and dressed early. We walked up the track from our house to the machine shop with Dad, watched him climb aboard a crew car, and watched the crew trains head out to the woods. I knew the engineers well. There was Mr. Foss Cox, who ran No. 3. He had two sons, Merton and Wilbur, who were just about my age, maybe a little older. Then there was Mr. Joe Liebentritt, who ran the One-Spot. Mr. L, as Mother called him, lived in the little house next to ours that used to be the schoolhouse.

After the crew trains left, Mother and I walked over to No. 2, where Mr. Casey was oiling and tightening down grease cup caps in preparation for a busy day of work. Mother told him I wanted to be a locomotive engineer. Mr. Casey pulled a fancy railroad watch from a pocket in the bib of his overalls, checked the time, and then looked at me.

"Why don't you and your mother ride with us up to the siding?" he suggested. "We'll pick up a train of logs and talk." With Mr. Casey's help Mother and I climbed up into the cab. Mr. Casey motioned for me to stand by the cab window on his, the engineer's, side of the cab. George Paris, better known as Five-Fingered Frenchy, climbed up behind us. Frenchy was head brakeman on No. 2.

"Little Sam here wants to be an engineer," Mr. Casey told Frenchy. His eyes and his voice were serious. Mr. Paris seemed impressed.

"You got a good teacher," he said. "Jim's a top man on a throttle."

Mr. Casey backed little No. 2 off the shop track and onto the main line. The second brakeman lined up the switch and No. 2 was ready for work.

Mr. Casey set me in a kneeling position on the engineer's seat. He pushed the heavy Johnson bar forward so the steam in the cylinders would make us move ahead. He told me to put both hands on the throttle bar. He rested his big left hand next to mine.

"Now pull," he said, "pull hard."

Mr. Ward had everything ready for my initiation as a locomotive engineer. Little No. 2 shook with the rumble of flame in its firebox. The engine bell clanged a warning that we were about to move. Little No. 2 was only a forty-two-ton engine but suddenly it seemed as big as Fog Mountain. I gripped the throttle firmly and watched smoke and hot steam swirling around the stack.

Above the roar of the firebox I could hear Mother's voice. "Do as Mr. Casey said, Samuel. Pull the throttle. Pull hard."

Suddenly I was just a small boy at the throttle of a giant machine. Tears welled from what moments before had been ecstatic eyes.

"I can't," I cried. "I can't. I'm scared."

I could feel Mr. Casey's big hand tighten on the throttle and then pull. Little No. 2 seemed to take a deep breath as steam seeped into its cylinders. Then with a sharp bark from its stack it moved. There was another bark and it moved faster.

"You did it, you are running the locomotive," cried Mother.

Mr. Casey and I knew better. It was he who was gently pulling the throttle bar. My hands were holding on tightly but doing no work. I turned my head so I could see Mr. Casey. He gave the tiniest nod of understanding and just the trace of a smile. I know my eyes must have mirrored my gratitude.

There was no doubt in my mind. What Mr. Paris had said

had to be true. Mr. Jim Casey was undoubtedly the very best locomotive engineer in the whole world.

We rode up to the storage track where the loaded log cars were held and waited while No. 2 hooked onto its train. With everything checked and ready, it eased out onto the main line and began its ten-mile trip to the log dump at Olney. Mother and I had decided to walk the quarter of a mile back to camp.

"There are many kinds of engineer," she remarked as we walked along the track, stepping from tie to tie and keeping our eyes down to avoid tripping on the rock ballast. "You wouldn't have to be a locomotive engineer," she added. "You could be a civil engineer and build things such as railroad lines, lay out logging camps, plan bridges. Your father and I think you would make a very fine civil engineer."

I realized then that when she had first told Dad I had the makings of a good engineer she wasn't referring to a locomotive engineer or a donkey engine man. All along she had in mind a civil engineer, one of those men who went out into the woods with transits and maps and measuring tapes and spent a lot of time in the office.

I was certain I didn't want to be that kind of an engineer but I didn't tell Mother. I was too busy thinking of Mr. Casey and little No. 2. The next time he would put me in the engineer's seat I would grab that old throttle and pull.

Next time I wouldn't be scared. I would pull and pull until little old No. 2 would fairly roar. I would take a whole train of loaded log cars down to Olney all by myself.

Mr. Casey would be really surprised.

And Mother and Dad would be so proud.

And my good friend Rex Gaynor would be jealous as anything.

Because I would be the littlest boy in camp to really run a steam locomotive.

Someday I would have to tell Mother that I didn't want to be her kind of engineer.

7

Them Eye-talians

One of the novelties at the Western Cooperage Company's headquarters camp was Lena Boyle's piano.

Pianos were a rarity in the timber and farm country of Clatsop County. One reason there were so few was their size and weight. It was almost impossible to deliver one by team and wagon or chain-drive truck over the roads of that period. The only alternative was by boat from Astoria to Olney and by log train from Olney to the camp.

Lena was a Baumgartner girl. Mr. Baumgartner was a prosperous Olney rancher, so the Baumgartners had a piano. When Lena was married she got the piano. It was a heavy upright and on shipping day shared space on a flatcar with several reels of logging cables, a hundred or so boxes of dynamite, cookhouse and commissary supplies, and five ten-gallon cans of fresh milk from Mr. Holm's pickup platform that he had thoughtfully built for that very purpose beside the Western Cooperage tracks. As a result he supplied the camp families and cookhouse with milk.

The heavy reels of logging cables could be rolled from a loading platform onto a flatcar, but Lena Boyle's piano had to be lifted.

"What the hell has she got in this thing," Five-Fingered

Frenchy is said to have asked, "a Tommy Moore block?" A Tommy Moore block was a heavy logging block (pulley) used in the woods. A piano like Lena's would weigh around seven hundred pounds. The train crew finally got it on the flatcar and anchored with rope.

Mr. Casey said Frenchy, using a box of dynamite as a piano stool, played his five-fingered version of chopsticks the entire ten-mile trip to camp. (Frenchy had lost his fingers in the days of link-and-pin couplings on railroad log cars.)

Getting Lena's piano to camp, it turned out, was the easy part. It took Dad, Mr. Robinson, Uncle Marsh, and Mr. Boyle, plus Frenchy and the other train brakeman, to get it into the Boyle house. Dad said it was so heavy it almost tipped the house off its log skids. Mother said he was exaggerating just because he had to help bring a little refinement to camp.

Marguerite Pinnell, the camp schoolteacher at the time, was a passable player. Lots of evenings camp families would crowd into Lena's house for an evening of entertainment. Miss Pinnell would play folk songs and the rest of us would sing. We called it singing but some loggers who would go to bed right after supper had other names for it. Mother used to sing in the church choir when she was in Boston and had a good voice. A new bride in camp, Mrs. Bob Ziak, had an astounding voice. It was deep but "operatic," as Mother described it. Mrs. Johnson sounded like a foghorn and one time when she lost her place on the sheet music I heard her mumble, "Bullshit." Mother was singing so loud she didn't hear it, and that was a good thing because if she had she might have sent me home and to bed.

Jim and Rose Casey liked to sing and so did Daddy O'Hoyt. Mr. O'Hoyt would often bring up a couple of bottles of his homemade dandelion wine. After a glass or two of that, Uncle Marsh and Dad would often boom out. Mrs. O'Hoyt didn't sing. Sometimes we kids would say words but mostly we just stood around and watched.

Word got around camp that Mother could play the piano.

Miss Pinnell was good on folk songs but she wasn't much on two-steps and that kind of dance music.

After a few snorts of Daddy O'Hoyt's dandelion wine one night Mrs. Johnson yelled out, "Caroline, set down at the pianner and give us some foot-stompin' music." Mother said all she could play was religious hymnal music and she couldn't play that very well.

"What's good enough for the Lord is good enough for us," persisted Mrs. Johnson. Mother demurred. The others insisted. Miss Pinnell got up from the stool and motioned for Mother to play. She didn't want to but she finally did. She spoke the truth when she said she wasn't very good but she was my mother and I was proud of her.

I don't remember the several songs she played but I recall the first one. It was "Little Brown Church in the Vale." I thought maybe Mrs. Johnson would give us a dance. But she just stood and listened and so did the others. Pretty soon Mrs. Ziak began singing the words and then so did Miss Pinnell. Then for some reason or other all the women had tears in their eyes.

Aunt Blanche spoke up. "We need a church in this camp," she said.

Mrs. Johnson nodded. "We sure as hell do."

The church idea never did materialize but sometimes on Sundays some of the families would go over to Lena and Eddie Boyle's. Mother would play hymns and the rest would sing.

But Mother did help organize a Sunday school. Mrs. Johnson promised she would send her Fen and Jake. They played hooky one Sunday and when Mrs. Johnson found out she went to work on them with a piece of cedar shake. Both boys were bawling like lost calves and Mrs. Johnson was puffing when she finished.

"You do that again," she warned, "and you'll have a blister the size of a belly pad on your hinder." I don't know how much Fen and Jake learned at Sunday school but they never missed another session.

Mother asked about a "belly pad."

"Caroline," said Mrs. Johnson, shaking her head in pain at such ignorance, "didn't you learn anything in that Boston school?" Mother said there were no better schools than those in Boston even if they had overlooked the meaning of "belly pad."

"A belly pad," sighed Mrs. Johnson with a resigned look, "is a hot cake. Now don't tell me they don't have hot cakes in Boston!" Mother said they did but they called them hot cakes.

Marguerite Pinnell got along fine with the camp people and she was a good teacher. Dad voiced the opinion one evening at supper that the camp was lucky to get such a good teacher. And one that was good-looking to boot.

The part about her being a good teacher *was* luck, Mother agreed, but the good-looking part resulted from a careful screening by Mr. Soderback and the other male members on the District 25 school board.

"They aren't interested in anyone over twenty-one who wears glasses or doesn't have a figure," bristled Mother.

"To be a good teacher a woman doesn't have to look like a female porcupine," said Dad. He realized too late he shouldn't have said that. Right while Mother was lecturing to him he got up and went outside. If I had done a thing like that I would have gotten a spanking.

The Western Cooperage board did seem to lean toward younger, nice-looking women. Miss Pinnell was nineteen when she came to teach. Miss Edith Hoskins was eighteen. I had her when I was in the fourth grade. By that time there were only two pupils in school, Howard Tate and I. Howard was in the eighth grade and was only about four years younger than Miss Hoskins. Howard's dad was Mel Tate, engineer on the Four-Spot, a rod engine that in 1917 replaced the little Two-Spot Shay as the Western Cooperage Company's main-line engine. I cried when that happened but Mother said God would look out for little No. 2 and see that it found a good home. It did. It was sold to a timber firm in Washington and then came to Oregon again, where it worked for three different outfits until 1953, when it was retired to a park where kids like my grandkids can study and admire it.

I liked both Miss Hoskins and Miss Pinnell. I had Miss Pinnell in the second grade and she was the only one who ever gave me 100 in deportment. That was important because right on our report cards there was printing that said, "Deportment should always be 100." Mother always looked at deportment. Miss Della Brown, my first grade teacher, wrote right on my card: "Relies too much on others" and "Whispers too much." Rex Gaynor and I put live polliwogs in her water bucket. I took Miss Pinnell a trillium when they came into bloom in late March and early April.

I think it was 1918 when Mother and Dad bought a phonograph. It was the first one in camp and my, but Mother was proud of it. We bought it through a Mr. Kienle who was a soldier assigned to work in the office with the Spruce Division during the war. His folks had a music store in Newberg, which is way over by Portland. That was a long way from our camp but things like phonographs were scarce in wartime so you bought one where you could. He brought it back with him on the back seat of his car clear from Newberg when he went there one time on a visit. It was a handsome cabinet talking machine and cost $125. On the inside of the lid that lifted up to expose the turntable and playing arm there was a picture of a dog listening to a table-size talking machine. It had the words: "His master's voice."

All the camp people came by to see it. Mr. Robinson's wife, Lucille, said it was so pretty that even if it wouldn't play it was worth the price.

But it did play. Mr. Kienle wound up the big spring and put a steel needle in the playing-arm head. Then he asked what should be the first record. I knew the one I wanted. Dad and Mother had ordered "Chicken Little." On the other side was "Goldilocks and the Three Bears."

" 'Chicken Little,' " I shouted from my rocking chair.

Mother said "Shhhhh" to quiet me down and told me to stop rocking so hard or I would throw the needle off the record. Then she nodded to Mr. Kienle.

" 'Chicken Little,' " she said.

Mr. Kienle was an awful fuss-budget. He had to dust and do some other things. I thought he would never get the record on the little center thing that stuck up above the turntable. I was so excited that if something didn't happen real quick I knew I would wet my pants.

He finally got the record in place, released the turntable and suddenly there it was, the voice of Georgene Faulkner telling the story of Chicken Little. Mother could tell the story better than the Faulkner lady, there was no doubt, but the wonder was that there was a human voice coming right out of a big box. One thing that pleased me was that now with our talking machine I could hear "Chicken Little" whenever I was ready. Even when Mother was busy getting supper, or baking bread, or making doughnuts or cookies. The record cost $1.25 and I still have it. Miss Faulkner would never know how many hours of pleasure she brought me way out in Oregon in a remote Coast Range logging camp.

And I'll bet she never dreamed that next to me her biggest admirer was probably Mrs. Johnson.

One day after listening to an overdose of opera ending with excerpts from *Il Trovatore* sung by Louise Homer and Enrico Caruso, Mrs. Johnson got fed up.

"Caroline," she groaned, "don't that damn machine talk anything but Eye-talian?"

Mother said it did and to prove it put on "Chicken Little." It was the first time Mrs. Johnson had heard the story and she was enthralled. Sitting in Dad's big chair, she rocked, puffed on her corncob pipe, and listened. After several playings Mother turned the record over to "Goldilocks and the Three Bears." Mrs. Johnson was upset by an obvious tall tale.

Caroline Snow Churchill holding young Samuel Churchill.

The Sam Churchill family in the Oregon big woods in 1914. Big
Sam, Little Sam, and Caroline.

Uncle Marshall Churchill and Aunt Blanche after their marriage in 1912.

The Oregon country in Clatsop County as Caroline Snow Churchill saw it in 1911. The river in the foreground is Youngs River, up which she sailed in the little launch *Teddy Roosevelt* as a bride from Boston. The camp to which she went was to the left of Saddle Mountain, the 3,300-foot peak in the left background.

Western Cooperage Company's headquarters camp near Astoria, Oregon, about 1917. Mrs. Johnson lived in the tent house at the right behind the big stump.

This home of locomotive engineer Jim Casey and his family was typical of Oregon logging camp homes in the early 1900s. (*Photo courtesy of Mrs. George W. Brunner*)

"Whoever heard of bears sleeping in beds and living in a house?" she challenged Mother. Mother was so dumfounded she stood stock-still with a bunch of bread dough in her hands. She finally stammered that she guessed Mrs. Johnson was right. She never had heard of bears sleeping in houses. She put the dough back in the mixing dish, wiped her hands, and flipped the record back to "Chicken Little."

Mrs. Johnson settled back in Dad's chair, relit her pipe, and listened.

"It's like I tell my Fen and Jake," she intoned to Mother, "it don't pay to tell lies."

Mrs. Johnson's reaction to "Goldilocks and the Three Bears" upset Mother.

"You don't suppose she was having a little fun with me, do you?" she asked Dad at supper. Mother had a quick mind and, when she was irritated, a rapier tongue. But she was notoriously slow in grasping the punch line of a joke or recognizing even Dad's wry type of humor.

"When it comes to Mrs. Johnson," Dad comforted her, "there is no telling what she is up to. Anyone that can sit and listen to 'Chicken Little' oughtn't to be upset by a bear story." Noticing me, he added, "I mean grownups, Samuel."

Our talking machine posed other questions for Mrs. Johnson. She wondered if Enrico Caruso, the great tenor, was any relation "to Robinson Caruso who got shipwrecked on a desert island." Mother just sighed and said she didn't think so. Mrs. Johnson was also curious about opera singer Alma Gluck.

"Where in God's name would a body get a name like that?" she asked Mother.

"From her father, I suppose," answered Mother. Mrs. Johnson mulled that over for a moment, then brightened. Smiling, she started humming a little rhyme that apparently had just occurred to her: "Alma Gluck needs a f—"

Mother interrupted Mrs. Johnson's reverie with a frantic "Mrs. Johnson!" Mrs. Johnson cut off the last word and grinned.

"I wouldn't have said it," she chortled, pleased at Mother's panicked reaction.

Mrs. Johnson loved our talking machine and so did many others in camp but Mrs. Bob (Kate) Ziak probably enjoyed it the most. She and Mother would listen to opera records by the hour. She had heard her favorites so many times that sometimes she would pick up parts of an aria and sing it along with the music.

"The woman is fantastic," Mother would tell Dad. "Absolutely fantastic. If she lived in Boston she would surely be taking voice lessons. She should be on the stage."

Mr. Ziak and Dad worked together a lot. He was as big as Dad and just as powerful. Mother always said that with Dad and Uncle Marsh pushing and Bob Ziak pulling, the three of them could outperform a donkey engine.

Mother always called Mrs. Ziak "girl." I guess it was because she was young, beautiful, and a bride. When her first baby was due the camp women gave her a shower and Mother wrote a little poem. It was cute and it was the only time I know of that Mother tried her hand at poetry.

In later years Mrs. Ziak did take music lessons from an Astoria teacher. I felt sorry for her having to go to school but Mother said singing was much like being a locomotive engineer. You had to have training.

Between Lena Boyle's piano and our Victor talking machine the Western Cooperage headquarters camp was getting a reputation for music and dances. Dancing was a popular form of entertainment with logging camp people and they would go far distances just to dance all night, eat, and be home in time to go to work. Mr. Casey was a good hand with the violin and Clay Clark, who lived near us, could play the banjo. Sophia Harrison from down at the Potter and Chester camp, three miles below us, could play the piano. The three of them used to play for the Olney dances.

Olney dances were most every Saturday night. Loggers and

their wives used to come for miles around. The dances were held in the attic of a warehouse. The parents would bed down the kids in blankets spread on the floor at one end of the building. When the dance started it steamed right through to dawn. There were always plenty of fights, ending in lots of black eyes, sore jaws, and bruised knuckles, but nobody ever got mad. It was just logger exuberance, according to Aunt Blanche. Mother never approved of physical encounters of any kind but with Dad she didn't have much to worry about, and neither did Aunt Blanche. Dad and Uncle Marsh were so big and strong they could usually avoid a fight simply by grabbing an overly zealous merrymaker and shaking the "exuberance" right out of him.

About midnight the dancers would call an intermission and everyone would go over to Mrs. Olson's hotel for sandwiches, coffee, and sweets. Revitalized, the dancers were then ready to whirl, clomp, and argue until dawn. About the time the morning sun peeked over the eastern ridges the music stopped, any sleeping kids were gathered up, and back we went to Mrs. Olson's hotel for breakfast.

Later in the day, after players and spectators had sobered up a bit, there would be a baseball game. Most of the camps, including the Western Cooperage, had baseball teams. Umpires were picked for their size and brawling ability. The ball game fights were usually more interesting than the games and Uncle Marsh was usually in the middle of things. When no one else would umpire Uncle Marsh would give it a try. He really didn't know a ball from a strike, but as Mike O'Farrell, the Olney pitcher, used to say, a disgruntled player had to be either drunk or a stranger to argue.

Olney also had a women's baseball team. Mike O'Farrell's sister, Rose, was the pitcher. She worked in the office at Potter and Chester's and could also play the piano. She would ride her horse the seven miles from camp to Olney to play ball, dance, or visit her folks.

Grange halls hosted most of the Saturday night dances, but

when roads were bad or there was snow on the ground, logging camp cookhouses and even private homes were substituted. With Mr. Casey, Clay Clark, and Miss Pinnell, the Western Cooperage folks rarely had to waste a Saturday night, no matter what the weather. Eager hands would push back the cookhouse tables and benches to clear a spot for dancing, and as quickly as Mr. Casey could get his fiddle tuned up, folks would be dancing.

If Mr. Robinson wouldn't open the cookhouse a few folks might drop in on Lena and Eddie Boyle, push back the furniture, and use Lena's piano. Or they might drop by our house and crank up our Victrola.

The various Spruce Division camps that housed soldier loggers to get out spruce timber for World War I aircraft frames also sponsored dances at intervals and invited women and girls from the area. There was a big spruce camp up the county road just a couple of miles from our camp. Mother, Aunt Blanche, and other camp wives used to go to the Spruce Camp dances to act as chaperones and to dance. Older girls like Mae Casey and Zada Peets were always in demand. Mr. Casey usually was there with his fiddle.

There were also Saturday night dances at Vinemaple, Elsie, Jewell, and Birkenfeld and Mist. Jewell was the closest and even it was ten miles southeast from our camp over a torturous road. Birkenfeld and Mist were in Columbia County and almost impossible to get to, to go to a dance, unless a body left the Western Cooperage early in the morning. But there were folks who would go just to see some new faces, get a change of scenery, and enjoy watching someone else fight.

Sometimes when there was a dance at Vinemaple or Elsie a group from our camp would go. Vinemaple was about five miles beyond Jewell, and Elsie was beyond Vinemaple. The roads weren't good but they were better than from Jewell to Birkenfeld and Mist.

Sometimes when the snow was too deep for an auto or a team

64

and wagon the loggers would hire a team and sleigh to go to Vinemaple. Billy Deeds, who ran the stage between Astoria and Jewell, often played for the Vinemaple dances. Mr. Deeds could make a fiddle talk. Mother said the Vinemaple dances were worth the long, cold ride in winter because sometimes after the dance everyone would be invited over to the Dave Tweedle ranch for breakfast.

The Tweedles' big farm table would be loaded down with Tweedle ham, Tweedle bacon, Tweedle eggs, Tweedle milk, Tweedle sausage, and Tweedle butter in addition to platters of hot cakes, hot biscuits, syrup, honey, and even mush if you wanted it. Everyone chipped in and helped but most of the food came from the Tweedle larder. Mr. Tweedle was the one who raised hogs and fattened a lot of his pigs at the Western Cooperage where he could get free leftovers from the cookhouse. The Tweedles appreciated loggers, especially those at the Western Cooperage.

Usually the sun was wide awake by the time the dancers finished one of those Tweedle breakfasts. The women would help clear the tables, wash the dishes, and get the house back in order while the men would rest up for the ball game, or trout-fish in the nearby Nehalem River, or help Mr. Tweedle with his morning chores.

Mother was always pleased with the co-operative spirit and eagerness to help but Mr. Tweedle, though appreciative and good-natured about it, was less enthusiastic. He told Mother that the Sunday after a Saturday night dance at Vinemaple was invariably a poor milk day for his dairy cows. The reason was that the eager but playful loggers always wanted to milk but their milking sessions usually ended up in milk fights with the men squirting milk in every direction but the bucket. They also loved to feed the dozen or more cats that were always around at milking time looking for handouts.

I guess the cows weren't overly pleased. To begin with, as Dad explained it, no cow could be "contented" with strange hands grabbing her teats and pawing around her udders. Mr. Tweedle told Mother that Dad and Uncle Marsh were good milkers and if they ever wanted to go back to the farm there would be a job at his place.

The exuberance, drive, and stamina of loggers at the Saturday night dances always amazed Mother. She could never understand how men whose jobs took such physical effort could have energy left over at the end of the day for fun-and-game things such as dancing, women, and sex.

"Don't loggers ever get tired and just sit down and rest, or read a book?" she asked Mrs. Robinson. Mrs. Robinson said, rarely. She said the very nature of a logger's work—the constant danger, the noise, the power and the size of the machines he worked with—made relaxation a luxury he never could really afford.

She likened a logger to one of nature's wild creatures. Even at rest every muscle and nerve was alert. The instinct for survival never slept. If it did the penalty could be death.

It was all pretty disconcerting to Mother. She had never really thought much about the dangers of Dad's work. Her talk with Mrs. Robinson explained a lot of things. It explained Uncle Marsh's devil-may-care attitude; it explained the exuberance and pleasure exhibited at every Saturday night dance; it explained, in part, the logger's love of booze, women, and sin. But it didn't explain how Dad could sleep with Mother screaming and a cougar on the roof.

Dad was now forty-seven and one of few his age still dodging snapping lines, logs, and falling snags in the Western Cooperage woods.

"Sam," Mother asked Dad one night at supper, "have you ever considered quitting the rigging and maybe taking a job in the machine shop?"

Dad said he hadn't.

"Would you?" pressed Mother.

"Nope," said Dad.

"Why not?" asked Mother.

"Because they'll be plenty of time for that when old age and rheumatism catch up with me," said Dad.

Dad could be mighty stubborn about some things. But so could Mother.

Dad didn't know it but he was already on his way to the Western Cooperage machine shop.

Mother and Mrs. Robinson had seen to that.

8
Follow the Tracks

Everything at the Western Cooperage camp centered around the logging railroad track.

All of the heavy equipment used in the logging operation came in from the log dump at Olney by train. A new steam donkey engine would arrive on a heavy steel flatcar called a moving car. Its first stop would be the machine shop, where crews would make the necessary checks and servicing to put it in operating condition. The big machine and its crew of servants never wanted for an audience while undergoing its preliminary work. There were always small boys on hand to watch and ask questions.

During our first year at the new headquarters camp mail also came in by train. The heavy canvas mail pouches, locked and sealed by Astoria post office employees, were a highlight of the day and a source of anticipation. They would contain letters from the East for Mother, sometimes letters from Dad's relatives in Maine, and always magazines, newspapers, and now and then packages. Near Christmas was when the packages would really come. A lot of them would be from Montgomery Ward and Sears, Roebuck and contain gifts and other items ordered from those two mail order houses.

The Christmas package rush always seemed to irritate Mr. Bramble, who besides doing the company bookkeeping work and supervising the commissary had to open the mail pouches and distribute the mail.

He would break the seals and open the locks on the heavy canvas sacks and then upend them and dump their contents on the office floor. Then he would read off the names on the various pieces in the pile. If you were there you would reach out and he would hand it to you. If you were absent he would lay your letters and stuff aside.

Mr. Bramble would permit no interfering with his delivery routine. I remember Mother one time reaching toward the pile for a letter from her sister Sue. Mr. Bramble got very upset.

"You don't reach out and grab a letter," he chastised Mother. "This is United States mail and I am responsible for it."

Mother's letter was lying there, face up on the pile, but Mr. Bramble ignored it. He picked up letters on all sides of it and would call the names but stubbornly refused to reach for Mother's. Mother's blood pressure was rising but she didn't want to make a scene and she wasn't going to give Mr. Bramble the satisfaction of having her beg. Mother bit her lip and held out, but it was too much for Mrs. Robinson.

"Oh, for chrissake, Sharkey," she growled, "give Caroline her letter." Mr. Bramble acted as though he hadn't heard her. Mrs. Robinson wasn't one to put up with being ignored. She reached out, snapped the letter from the pile, and handed it to Mother.

"You can't do that," shouted Mr. Bramble. "That's United States mail."

"I can do any damn thing I want," snarled Mrs. Robinson. "My husband is superintendent of this camp and if I want to pick a letter out of that pile I'll pick it. Now, what are you going to say to that?"

Never before had I seen Mrs. Robinson so wrought up. And there wasn't much Mr. Bramble could say. Mrs. Robinson wasn't one to throw her weight around but when she had to she

69

could. One time when we were up at the Robinsons' for an evening she told about the time she was a secretary-treasurer for a mining company in Nome, Alaska, and was delivering a payroll by boat when the boat sank. She and several men drifted on a raft almost to Siberia before they were rescued. She was real proud that when they were rescued she still had the payroll money. She was thirty-one, a handsome woman, and loved the outdoors. Her brother, Oscar Ward, was fireman for Mr. Casey on the Two-Spot, my favorite locomotive. Mother and Mrs. Robinson got along first rate, and if you had a problem you could always go to Mrs. Robinson and she would listen and help if she could.

Mr. Robinson always said that Lucille ran the house and he ran the camp. One time when the Robinsons were down to our house for supper T.W. made that statement. Dad nodded in agreement but I thought I saw Mrs. Robinson wink at Mother and Mother wink back. I asked her about it later after the Robinsons had gone home. Mother looked startled for a moment but then she smiled, patted my head, and said I must have been mistaken. But I knew I wasn't. I can tell when a person winks.

Mother seemed to be fascinated by railroad tracks. The Western Cooperage Company's railroad was no marvel of perfection. Mother admitted it was no Union Pacific but it represented the skills and talents of a lot of men. Our camp was surrounded by some of the roughest terrain around and it always was a source of wonder to Mother how loggers who weren't trained engineers could blast through rock cliffs, bridge gorges, and climb mountains to form a path of steel that locomotives could follow. In later years the company did employ a trained location engineer whose job was to survey railroad routes and keep grades at a minimum. But for many years a lot of Western Cooperage railroad was built by men like Dad and Uncle Marsh who didn't even have a grammar school education.

When we first moved to the company's headquarters camp the railroad was not only our link with the outside—it was the barometer of how things were progressing at the logging end; it was the arterial that took us on exciting exploration trips; it was an adventure trail and a recreation path; it would have made a dandy sled slide in winter but none of us kids had a real smooth sliding "flyer" with steel runners. The grade through camp was just enough so that on a real factory sled we would probably have coasted all the way to Olney and had to wait until spring to get home.

Camp people seemed to like to live near the railroad. Women and children used to gather on porches or in yards to watch the trains go by. A long train of big, rich-looking Douglas fir logs with bark sometimes almost a foot thick indicated the big machines and their crews were working without interruption and paychecks at the end of the month should be good. Short trains or trains of scrubby-looking timber indicated the men were in a poor show, work was hard, and results were minimal.

In addition to mail, food, and supplies, the logging railroad delivered our wood supply. Usually in late summer several cars of wood logs would be brought to camp and the logs would be rolled off the cars onto cleared areas near loggers' homes. The best stovewood was from a Douglas fir log because it was straight-grained and easy to split and didn't throw sparks like spruce or hemlock. Once the logs were delivered the fathers would go to work on them with crosscut saws, cutting them into the proper lengths for a stove. The big circular blocks were then split into stovewood and piled in woodsheds for winter storage and use. A log four or five feet in diameter would provide one family with enough wood to last through the winter. In the event there was a miscalculation or a winter with above-normal snow and cold most of the camp fathers had a reserve wood supply tucked away to fall back on. Dad was one of those who kept a close watch on the woodshed. If our supply seemed to be going down faster than he expected he would take my homemade sled and, with me along for company, would cut a supply of alder. Even on these forage trips the railroad track was our trail. It took only a few inches of snow to cover the ties and rock ballast and provide a fairly smooth path for the sled.

Alders thrived along Klaskanine Creek and sometimes crept in close to the tracks. Dad would select trees six to eight inches in diameter, fall them, and cut them into cookstove and heating stove sizes with his double-bit ax. Seasoned alder produced a hot fire but it burned quickly. The winter alder was fairly green but it would burn and help save the better Douglas fir for cooking.

Metal strips on my sled may have been a good idea in theory but didn't work in practice. A lot of camp supplies came in wooden barrels, which meant there were metal barrel hoops in abundance. Dad cut a couple of metal hoops into long strips and nailed them to the bottom of the sled runners. The idea was to make the runners slip more easily over snow. The problem was the barrel hoops were rusty and instead of slipping they gripped like sand. With a load of alder on the sled it was all Dad and I could do to move it, even on frozen snow. Dad would pull and I would push but with his long legs and bigger steps he usually ended up pulling both the sled and me. If he noticed he never said anything. It was his way of having me participate in family activities. Usually after a couple of trips Mother would have a kettle of hot cocoa for us and Dad would suggest we go inside for a brief spell, warm our hands, and have some hot cocoa.

Those moments were very precious because Dad and Mother were accepting me as almost a grownup and in my heart I was certain I had earned the honor.

Spring was a marvelous time along the railroad tracks. You could walk along and day by day see nature coming alive after a long winter's sleep. There was always color in our land even in the dead of winter. The coniferous trees retained their greens, of course, as did sword fern, a variety of mosses, some grasses, and the bark of young alder. The land was never dull and bleak as in areas where winter strikes hard with vicious cold and heavy snows.

Some years the hardier plants would have color until late in

October and alder would often hold many of its leaves even into November. December and January were the real winter months. Of course, we did have the rains, which often began in October and seemed to last well into March and sometimes April.

But as early as late February daffodils would be in bloom, their yellow faces mirroring the glory that was to come.

Usually by late February there were other stirrings. Alder tips would be showing traces of green, skunk cabbage with its pungent odor and yellow floral stalk was open for inspection. In March the pussy willows were out and in April the bright yellow Johnny-jump-ups dotted the greening expanse of the land, the alder was leafing out, and salmonberry was in the green bud stage, soon to be followed by its handsome, shy lavender flowers, the forerunner of breakfast berries. One of the most exciting events in April was the blooming of trilliums. To us they were Easter lilies and their arrival always sparked a desperate rush to the darker recesses of the forest in search of the first trilliums to take to our mothers and to school and the teacher.

The Easter lily was one of Mother's favorite flowers. In favorable seasons these lilies could bloom as early as March, but whenever they appeared they were welcome. Their fragile ivory petals held high in noble bearing above the cluster of three leaves at the top of the main stem were regal to see.

Mother referred to them as wake-robins and they never failed to thrill her.

"It is a shame to steal from nature something so beautiful," she remarked one time when I delivered an especially large and beautiful trillium to her that I had found growing in moss cover at the foot of a huge Douglas fir. "But I do accept it and I love you for it." She leaned over and kissed my troubled face.

"But I didn't steal it, Mother," I told her. "It was just growing there waiting for me. I know it was waiting for me."

Mother saw the hurt in my eyes, read the dejection in my voice.

"I shouldn't have said 'steal,' " she said, reprimanding herself

73

and comforting me. "God did put that particular trillium there and I do honestly believe He put it there for you to find and give to me." She held me at arm's length and looked into my eyes with a troubled expression on her face. "When I said 'steal,'" she continued, "I just meant that all flowers, but particularly wake-robins, are so delicate and genteel it sometimes seems a shame to take them from nature, who has worked so hard to produce them. Do you understand?"

I didn't really but I nodded and Mother smiled that nice, comforting smile that always seemed to make everything, even a bad hurt, feel all right. But ever after when it was trillium time in the Western Cooperage forest I always asked her before I went trillium hunting if she would like me to pick one for her.

Her answer was always, "If God wants me to have a trillium He will show you where to look. If you find it I would love to have you bring it to me." I guess God really wanted Mother to have one of the first trilliums every spring because I was always among the first to find one.

By May and June the open areas in and around the camp were a garden of color with everything from buttercups to foxgloves and dandelions bursting free from their winter's sleep.

And it wasn't only flowers. There were thousands of tiny bugs and insects. Crawly things and things on the wing. Beneath every piece of rotted wood there was a colony of life.

Picking up an old board, Mother pointed out the mass of tiny creatures hustling about.

"Each of those is a creature of God," she stressed, urging me to get down on my knees and look close. She said each little body was a mass of living cells just like mine. It had feelings and could hurt the same as I did when I got bumped or pinched. Each, she said, had a job to do. It had the responsibility of preserving the species, providing food and shelter for its young, and contributing to the betterment of the earth.

"When they die will they go to heaven?" I asked.

Mother nodded. "Bugs, birds, trees, frogs, everything that

74

lives," she said, "is a part of God and when its work here is done it will go to heaven."

"Will you and Dad go to heaven?" She nodded.

"Will Mrs. Johnson?" She paused a fraction of a second, then smiled.

"Mrs. Johnson will go to heaven," she assured me.

"She cusses something fierce," I reminded her.

"I know," she said, shaking her head, "but when a person is kind and generous deep inside, God doesn't always base His judgment on what they say. He is guided by what they do."

When I told Jake and Fen Johnson what my mother had said about God and their mother and how God judges people by their actions as well as their words, neither expressed much interest.

"If Ma's layin' a switch to my bare ass is goin' to help her get to heaven I s'ppose I ought to be happy," philosophized Jake, "but I ain't." Fen nodded.

"If I had my druthers," he observed wryly, "I'd rather have Ma talkin' than actin'."

I got a better insight into their meaning a few days later when Mrs. Johnson was over at our house. Miss Pinnell was there too. It was my nap time but I wasn't sleepy. I fussed, stamped my feet on the linoleum, and said I didn't want to go to bed.

Mrs. Johnson was sitting in Dad's big rocker and rocking. Mother stepped outside to fill the teakettle at the water pipe and while she was gone Mrs. Johnson leaned forward and whispered, "If you was my little boy do you know what I would do?"

"What?" I asked between sobs.

"I'd get me a good switch and lay it right across your bare ass."

When Mother came in with the kettle of water I was tucked in my cot and eager for my nap. Mother took note and sounded pleased.

"Samuel sometimes fusses at nap time," she admitted, "but I have learned that patience usually wins out."

Mother had the knack of weaving an object lesson into just about anything from the burbles of Klaskanine Creek to the big, cottony clouds that often floated across the Oregon summer sky. Even the Western Cooperage's logging railroad wasn't exempt.

One of her favorites was likening the railroad with its main line and spur lines to life.

"Without the railroad little No. 2 would wander all about the hills and canyons and never reach its destination," she remarked one day on one of our "track walks." She said the railroad provided a path and gave direction and purpose to the log trains. She said God, education, and parents did the same for little boys in real life.

"Dad and I are here to help get you started building your own railroad that will help you reach goals," she said. "If you could be anything you wished, what would you wish to be?" she asked.

"The engineer on Mr. Casey's Two-Spot," I promptly answered.

I could sense she had other plans for me but for the present she accepted the Two-Spot. She then listed a lot of things I would have to learn before Mr. Casey, or the company, would let me run the Two-Spot. Things such as hand and lantern signals, all the parts of the Two-Spot, and how to maintain and repair them. She said I would have to know what every pipe and valve was for, be able to reline the firebox with brick, shim up loose bearings, anticipate how hard to apply the brakes on the various grades, and know when and where to apply oil and grease.

"Does Mr. Casey have to know all that?" I was perturbed that Mr. Casey hadn't mentioned some of this during our discussions about my being an engineer.

"All of that and much, much more," Mother assured me. "But no matter what you decide to be, it will take hard work and study," she added.

She said too many people wandered onto spur lines and ended up at a dead end. In that kind of a situation you either had to back up and start over on the main line or stay where you were with a job that maybe you didn't like. I could understand the dead-end bit on a spur line. Logging railroad spur lines were temporary pieces of track built to log a certain area. When the logging was done the rails and ties were removed and laid down again as another spur in another place.

"Be a main line," stressed Mother. "Being on a spur line is like changing jobs over and over. You can never settle down. You never can travel very far because spur lines are short and don't really go anyplace."

It all seemed rather complicated and I could see I was going to ask Mr. Casey a lot more questions. And I guess I did because one day Mother suggested that I give Mr. Casey a rest and stop, at least for a while, asking him questions.

"He said you wanted to know all about main lines and spur lines, grease cups, bearings, and hand signals," she said. "Curiosity is a valuable tool," she added. "Don't ever be afraid to ask questions." In some ways it didn't quite make sense. Mother was telling me to ask questions and when I asked Mr. Casey questions he asked Mother to ask me to stop. I mentioned that to her.

"Don't overwhelm people," she suggested. "Ask and then think about the answer. Questions should be like steps. You take them one at a time."

The next time Mr. Casey and I talked I asked him only one question: "Why did you tell my mother I ask too many questions?" We were standing beside the Two-Spot while it was taking on water and Mr. Casey was oiling some unseen part with a long-spouted oil can.

"Because you were all talk and no listen," he finally answered.

Mr. Casey's main line and Klaskanine Creek were excellent examples of planning and not planning. Klaskanine Creek flowed from above Camp 2 through our camp and on down to Youngs River near Olney. It wound back and forth, dillied and dallied, and made twelve or thirteen miles out of what for the railroad was a ten-mile route.

"The railroad was planned," explained Mother. "God let Klaskanine Creek find its own way." She said that was fair enough for creeks but not for railroads or little boys.

More and more I found myself thinking about planning and building railroads. I guessed maybe it could be fun, too. But not as much fun as being an engineer, I mean a locomotive engineer.

9
The Machine Shop

Made to order for a small boy in a logging camp during storm and rain periods in the winter months was the blacksmith and machine shop. To us at the Western Cooperage headquarters camp it was a combination toy shop, park, and recreation area.

"It is the most wonderful spot in the whole world for a small boy," wrote Mother to Sue French, a Boston friend. "I can think of no place in Boston, or any place but another logging camp, that can match it."

Mother's enthusiasm was shared by every youngster in camp including me, my close friend Rex Gaynor, Merton and Wilbur Cox, Phillip Peets, and others. Older boys such as Bert Hathaway, Bud Peets, and a couple of others had other things they would rather do such as meet some of the older girls in hideaway places out in the woods.

"I think the school board should do something about that," Mother suggested to Mrs. Johnson.

"If they's big enough they's old enough," shrugged Mrs. Johnson, "and I don't advise you talkin' to parents or speakin' out at school meetin's." Dad sided with Mrs. Johnson.

"Out here they's two things you don't try to change: sexin' and boozin'."

"But they are so young," protested Mother.

"If they's—" Mother cut him short. "I know," she said, "Mrs. Johnson already told me."

For us younger ones sex was still pretty much a mystery but the big forges, steam hammers, wheel-turning lathes, drill presses, and other equipment in the shop were not.

For me the shop was more interesting than ever because Dad was now there. He was a blacksmith helper assisting big, brawny Mr. Jacobson, who could turn a saw file into a knife or raw bar steel into a 150-pound pair of log-loading tongs. Mr. Jacobson, Dad, and all the others in the shop were very important people and could save the company a lot of money. A pair of loading tongs, for example, could cost almost one hundred dollars. Counting raw material and labor costs, Mr. Jacobson could turn out a pair for maybe sixty or seventy dollars.

Almost every tool and piece of rigging used in the woods could be duplicated in the shop, and many of them were. Aside from helping Mr. Jacobson, Dad's specialty was making chokers, straps, and other cable items used on the rigging. A choker was a long length of cable fitted with a sliding hook so it could be slipped over the end of a log. The other end was hooked onto the butt rigging and when the main line was tightened the choker tightened itself around the log and would hold it in a tight noose while the log was being pulled to the landing.

Chokers were subjected to great strain and the lives of rigging men depended upon their being properly made. Dad was an acknowledged expert.

"I'd rather bet five hundred dollars on one of Sam Churchill's chokers than one dollar on a sunny day in December," was how one rigging man described his confidence in Dad's work.

The heart of the machine shop was the big stationary steam engine with its pair of tremendous flywheels. The big engine, overseen by Daddy O'Hoyt (who also took care of the boiler), was hooked by a broad belt to a long steel shaft mounted on bearings and fastened high up on the roof supports. The long steel shaft, known as a line shaft, had belt pulleys along its length. Each pulley transferred power to a machine by belt. All the power equipment in the shop, from machine lathes to hacksaw units, got its power from the big stationary steam engine, which powered the line shaft, which powered the system of pulleys and belts.

Magical things could be accomplished in the shop. A big wheel lathe could hold a whole railroad car wheel in its grip while it cut a new flange to keep the wheel on the rail. Smaller lathes could turn steel rods into threaded bolts, add the precision touch to a donkey engine or locomotive part, cut a groove in a bar of metal for a lock key, or any number of things. A lathe man was a precisionist. He dealt in infinitesimal tolerances where the slightest error would mean a wasted piece of metal or an inferior replacement part.

The sounds and smells in the machine shop were rich and heady. There was the steady, rhythmic whooosh, whooosh of the stationary steam engine as steam entered and left its single, massive cylinder. There was the rumbling sound of the heavy steam hammer as it shaped cherry-red pieces of metal, fresh from a forge. There was the sizzle of hot metal dipped in water to temper and cool it. There were the smells of oils and grease, hot metal, and steam, and of burning coal, a special low-sulfur grade free of impurities and guaranteed to produce high temperatures.

On rainy days, of which there were many in the high Coast Range in winter, we younger boys would gather in the machine shop. Dad would build a fire for us in one of the idle forges. A little engine waste with oil on it served as a starter. A belt-driven blower would send a fountain of air up through the coal and in minutes the center of the forge would be a caldron of glowing coal and blue-hot flame.

A piece of scrap metal would be thrust into the flaming bed of coals and in a few minutes we would have our own red-hot piece of metal that we could lift from the forge, place on an anvil, and shape and pound to our heart's content. We soon learned to operate the drill press and the powered hacksaw that would saw its way through any size piece of metal and do it unattended.

If we tired of using a forge we could walk over to one of the lathes and see who could collect the longest curls of metal slivered from a piece of work by the lathe's cutting tool. Or we could watch an engine crew relining the firebox of a locomotive, or Mr. Casey shimming up some of the bearings in the line shaft of his Shay locomotive.

One time as the big stationary engine was about to be started after lunch Daddy O'Hoyt motioned for me to come over to where he was. He showed me a big wheeled valve and said it controlled the flow of steam to the engine. He asked if I wanted to start the engine.

I recalled my experience in the cab of little No. 2 with Mr. Casey, and what a frightening and mortifying experience it was when I lost my nerve and couldn't pull the throttle. But Daddy O'Hoyt's smiling face gave me confidence.

"Yes," I answered him.

He placed both my hands on the big valve wheel and told me to turn it counterclockwise slowly. The wheel turned hard at first but I managed it. I could hear high-pressure steam beginning to surge past the opening valve and into the cylinder. Suddenly there was a great sigh and the big flywheels moved ever so slightly. I turned the wheel a little more and there was motion. The heavy engine breathed faster and faster. Daddy O'Hoyt told me to stop turning the valve—the engine had reached its working speed. He then engaged the pulley clutch that ran the master belt that connected the engine and the line shaft. In moments the entire shop was a hive of flowing belts and moving machines.

Daddy O'Hoyt smiled with approval. "When I get too old for this job I'll tell T.W. about you," he said. In an instant he became my number two idol, just the width of a bobcat's eyelash behind Mr. Casey. The frustration, defeat, and shock to my ego suffered from the locomotive fiasco were forgotten, wiped out. I was free, my confidence restored, my faith rejuvenated.

"Next to running Mr. Casey's Shay I would like your job the best," I told Daddy O'Hoyt with solemn frankness and honesty.

Daddy O'Hoyt died in Astoria in 1946 at the age of one hundred years and four months. When I knew him in the camp he was already in his seventies, and had iron-gray hair and a mustache that flowed across his upper lip and drooped at the corners. He was an expert with steam and moonshine whiskey and his quality "moonshine," produced by a still in his chicken house, sparked many a rural dance to life.

For many years he was a locomotive engineer and before that spent years traveling the world as a factory representative for Allis-Chalmers Machinery Company. He supervised the installation of many public improvements, including the Hong Kong waterworks, so the camp people said.

His wife, Ida, was his second wife. She told Mother his first wife died in 1894 and that she and Mr. O'Hoyt were married in Vancouver, Washington, years later. She said he was born in Syracuse, New York, in 1845 and that his mother bought his way out of the Civil War. His father had come to the United States from Dublin, Ireland, and Daddy O'Hoyt throughout his life spoke with a slight brogue.

When Dad first brought Mother to the Western Cooperage Daddy O'Hoyt was already there running a donkey engine. He would have been sixty-six years old by then and as active as a young bear.

Even back then he had some strange likes and dislikes. He had a fetish for cleanliness and bathed regularly even if he had to do it in Klaskanine Creek. He started every workday with clean clothes from his long, black wool underwear that was a favorite with loggers to his socks and bib overalls.

He wouldn't eat turkey, chicken, or eggs but had a continuing hunger for bear meat, garlic, and castor oil. He took castor oil at intervals and could drink it right out of the bottle. It used to make me gag just to watch him.

"Hoyt," Mrs. Johnson grunted at him one Sunday afternoon when the O'Hoyts and some of the other Cooperage camp families were gathered down at the crossing sitting around and gossiping, "if a b'ar ever took out after you he'd be running knee-deep in castor oil and crap." (Mrs. Johnson never pronounced the "O" in "O'Hoyt.")

Daddy O'Hoyt was five feet eight inches, stocky, and tending toward a noticeable paunch. The moment Mother saw him she marked him down as the camp Santa Claus. He tried to beg off but she wouldn't hear to that.

"Forget yourself and think of the joy you can bring to these camp children," Mother soothed and manipulated. He finally gave in. Mother with the help of the other women made him a suit and attached tinkle bells on the arms and legs and in a row across his paunch.

They couldn't dig up any reindeer so he had to walk up the railroad track in the snow. You could hear the jingle of his bells two hundred yards away. He had a bulging red bag of cookies, hard candies, and small stocking gifts and each present had the recipient's name on it. Several young ones who were a little doubtful that there really was a Santa Claus became staunch and solid believers when Daddy O'Hoyt in his glorious outfit knocked on the door and came stomping in.

Almost every home he entered seemed to just happen to have a bottle of the O'Hoyt chicken house product and eager fathers were generous with their rewards for Santa. By the time he got to our house he was so jolly his ho-ho-ho's and ha-ha-ha's were waking up slumbering bears a half mile away in the forest.

He told Mother and Dad that I was going to make one hell of a fine machine shop engineer. When I heard that I knew he had to be Santa Claus because up until now the only people in the whole wide world who knew I had run the big stationary steam engine in the shop were Daddy O'Hoyt, Mother, Dad, and me.

After Santa left I couldn't wait to tell Mother that "Santa is just like God. He knows everything!"

Mother smiled, kissed me on the cheek, and said that he did.

Daddy O'Hoyt continued as Santa Claus at Christmas for two or three years and he brought happiness to a dozen or more little boys and girls. But his own life began to have problems. One of them was Mr. F. B. Tichenor, deputy U.S. marshal in Astoria. Mr. Tichenor was determined to find Daddy O'Hoyt's still. He did, eventually, and when he did he confiscated the still and destroyed the mash, and Daddy and Ida ended up having to pay a $500 fine.

After that Mr. Tichenor didn't have many friends around the Western Cooperage. Mrs. O'Hoyt said they would never again get caught having to borrow money to pay a fine to keep Mr. O'Hoyt out of jail. She said she would set aside a little from every sale and use it as a nest egg if they ever got arrested again. Mrs. O'Hoyt got sick all of a sudden and died. Just before she died she did her mightiest to whisper something to her husband but she was too weak. Daddy O'Hoyt couldn't make out the words. She died while still trying.

Daddy O'Hoyt said she must have been trying to tell him where she had hid the money they had been saving. Most everybody in camp helped him search everything from his house to holes in stumps, soft earth spots, and hiding places in trees. The money, if there really was any, was never found. Years later, after the Western Cooperage had reorganized and become Tidewater Timber Company, the old O'Hoyt house was torn down. Dad said he never had seen a house taken apart with so much love and tender care. It was actually dismantled piece by piece and a job that should have taken a couple of days took almost two weeks. Every little knothole was inspected but Ida took her secret to the grave and still has it.

The old Western Cooperage shop was later rebuilt into a bigger, more modern one that could handle big rod engines and all kinds of stuff. But it never had quite the charm of the old barnlike structure that Daddy O'Hoyt oversaw and where we Western Cooperage boys loved to gather on a rainy day.

The old camp has been gone for thirty-five years and the logging railroad that was our main thoroughfare is now a graveled forest road. The mellow call of locomotive whistles no longer drifts across ridges and tumbles through camp between canyon walls.

But the memories are there. Memories as rich and alive as though it all happened yesterday.

Memories like that of a Santa Claus in bib overalls letting me turn the valve that started the big steam engine that ran the shop where a young boy was always welcome.

10
Man's Best Friend

In cattle country the horse may have been man's best friend but in timber country it was the dog—at least, most dogs. The Johnsons' dog, Prince, was an exception. Prince was no prince. He was crafty, noisy, and given to slinking up behind an unsuspecting person and taking a nip at ankle or leg.

For some reason Prince shared Mrs. Johnson's dislike of Sharkey Bramble. On the other hand he took a cue from his mistress and was always friendly toward Mother. Since I seemed acceptable to both Mother and Mrs. Johnson, Prince included me in his narrow list of acceptables. Dad was a borderline case. Prince sensed Dad to be a gentle, friendly type but one who would put up with no nonsense. There was something about Dad that said, "I'll feed you if you are hungry, help you if you are lonely or ill, but if you ever take a bite out of me I'll heave your carcass right over the top of Fog Mountain." Dad and Prince seemed to understand each other. Mother said what they did was ignore each other.

Mr. Bramble, now, was different. He despised Prince and the whole Johnson family and the feeling was mutual.

"If that dog of yours ever nips me I'll fix him up with a lead muzzle," Mr. Bramble warned Mrs. Johnson one day when

she and Mother were at the company commissary. The term
"lead muzzle" was a new one to Mother.

"What's a lead muzzle?" she asked.

"A .30-.30 slug right between the eyes," snapped Mr. Bramble.
Mother was dumfounded and horrified. She had always as-
sociated premeditated killings of humans and domestic pets with
criminals or maniacs.

"You wouldn't really deliberately kill an animal just because
you disliked it," she said hopefully.

"I've killed bear that weren't half as mean as that Johnson
dog," responded Mr. Bramble. The color drained from Mother's
face. She looked at him just as she looked at me whenever I had
done something terribly wrong and was about to be engulfed in
tears and a lecture and maybe a woodshed session with Dad.
Mother's tears always brought on tears of my own. Her lectures
always got off onto the Bible, God, clean living, and do unto
others. But I preferred them to a woodshed session with Dad.
Sometimes I got both. It looked to me as though Mr. Bramble
was in for a real tongue-lashing but Mrs. Johnson intervened.

"I wouldn't give Bramble a drink of piss if he was dyin' of
thirst," she announced to both Mother and Mr. Bramble, "but if
Prince ever bit him I'd kill him myself." Mr. Bramble stared at
Mrs. Johnson with mouth agape. Mother gasped in dismay.

"Prince is your pet. He loves you. He trusts you. Killing him
would be despicable," she gritted. "I know you too well," she
added, groping for words that wouldn't seem to come; "I don't
think you would do what you say you would."

"I'd have to." Mrs. Johnson shrugged.

"But why?" asked Mother.

"Because," said Mrs. Johnson, "I don't want nothin' in my
house with that sonofabitch's blood in it." Her solemnity ended
in peals of laughter and a hearty thump on Mother's back with
the flat of her hand. The strange part was that even Mr. Bramble broke into a tight little smile. He'd look at Mrs. Johnson,
shake his head, smile, and mutter, "Jesus!"

88

That night at the supper table Mother told Dad about the commissary episode and how Mr. Bramble seemed to enjoy being the butt of one of Mrs. Johnson's ribald witticisms.

"I just don't understand that kind of humor," she said. Dad's reaction to Mother's problem was mixed. He said he could understand Mr. Bramble's feelings but on the other hand a little of Mr. Bramble's blood in a dog would probably poison the poor animal anyway, so you might just as well shoot it and spare it any misery.

Mother replied huffily that she was having some problems with Dad's humor, too. She closed the subject by saying she was opposed to such talk around me. It was just a lot of adult ranting to me. I wasn't certain about Mr. Bramble but I would have bet two mink skins against one skunk hide that Mrs. Johnson would die before she would shoot Prince and I would bet anything that Dad might turn Mrs. Johnson over his knee but he wouldn't take it out on Prince if Prince bit him.

Opposing Prince in the camp's love 'em or shoot 'em contest was Tag. Tag was a handsome bloodhound owned by Mr. Harry Slater. Mr. Slater was part Indian, lean and hungry-looking, and Dad said even with his calk shoes on, it was almost impossible to hear him walking in the woods. Mr. Slater was the company fire warden and when it wasn't fire season he kept an eye open in the woods for I.W.W. members. "I.W.W." stood for "Industrial Workers of the World." It was a firebrand type of unionism that espoused worker revolution, destruction of capitalism, and organization of all workers into one huge union. During World War I there were fears that I.W.W. men would set forest fires. Once when Mr. Casey's train went through camp someone had chopped "I.W.W." in great big letters along the length of the peak log on a railroad car with three big logs on it. The log told us there was at least one I.W.W. member in our camp and Mr. Robinson said he might do anything from setting a forest fire to dynamiting a trestle or driving long spikes into logs. Any metal hidden in a log could shatter the big band saws in sawmills as they screamed at high speed, cutting timbers the length of a log.

Mrs. Johnson said if she ever knew for sure a man was an I.W.W. she would take a shotgun to him, and if a gun wasn't handy she would sic Prince on him. Mother said that would serve an I.W.W. right because I.W.W. men were terrible men.

Anyway, with Mr. Slater and his dog, Tag, around, we all felt comparatively safe. Dad said Tag was a terrific tracker and if he ever picked up the trail of an I.W.W. he would follow the man until he treed him. I asked Mr. Slater what he would do if Tag treed an I.W.W. man. Would he shoot him? Mr. Slater said no. He said he would arrest him and take him to the county jail in Astoria. I said if it were me I'd shoot him and kill him just like our soldiers were doing to the Germans where the big war was. Mr. Slater said no matter where it happened, killing people wasn't right. Even in war.

Well, that just didn't make sense to me and I told Mother what Mr. Slater had said. Mother said Mr. Slater was a pacifist. She said that meant he didn't believe in fighting and killing. She said if there were more people like Mr. Slater there wouldn't be any wars and people all over the world would be like brothers. I told her I wouldn't want a mean old German for a brother. She said most German people were just like us. She said there were fathers and mothers and little boys and little girls and that most of them didn't like the war any more than we did. Now, that was a real strange thing to say. I knew for a fact that Mrs. Johnson hated Germans and so did Uncle Marsh. Aunt Blanche never said much and neither did Dad. Mother said Aunt Hetty in Canada married a German, and that was a real shock because they had been down to the camp to visit us and I liked Uncle Harold. It seemed impossible that he could be a German. Mother said there were lots of Germans just like Uncle Harold. Nice people who worked, loved America, and had families like anyone else. I knew it had to be true, otherwise Mother wouldn't have said it.

The Western Cooperage was a big camp by now and there were lots of women that could help a little boy with a problem, but whenever I needed help with Mother I still went to Mrs. Johnson.

To get to the Johnsons' from our house was no problem. The Johnson boys, Fen and Jake, and I had cut a path from our house to theirs through the salmonberry bushes. It was just big enough for us kids, but Mother and Mrs. Johnson began using it and then so did others until it got to be a grownups' path and wasn't much fun any more for us. But we still used it. The path opened up into a little clearing right by the county road bridge over Klaskanine Creek. The Johnson house, a half cedar-shake structure with a tent flap for a roof, sat by the creek.

When I entered the clearing from the path Mrs. Johnson was outside sweeping off the piece of hewn log that served as a step into the one-room tent house. Prince saw me coming through the brush and came over to investigate. When he saw it was me he wagged his tail and gave a little bark of welcome.

It was then that I saw Mr. Slater with Tag on a rope leash walking by on the county road. Prince saw them, too, and went running toward them, belly close to the ground and growling menacingly. When he got fairly close he began barking and showing his fangs in ugly snarls. Tag and Mr. Slater paid no attention and just kept walking along. Prince kept his distance but continued his barking and snarling. I called to him to come back but he didn't. Mr. Slater looked up and waved to me.

Fen and Jake, hearing the commotion, came outside to see what was going on. As I have said before, they didn't like Tag and were always bragging that in a fight their Prince would chew him to pieces. There was agreement among the camp people that sooner or later Prince and Tag would fight it out to the death. Mr. Slater always kept Tag on a leash during their walks but he was a man with pride and Prince was always there to harass them during their walks.

"One of these days Harry is going to turn Tag loose and then you are going to see one hell of a fight," Uncle Marsh predicted. Dad said if he were a betting man he would bet on Prince. Uncle Marsh said he was a betting man and he would bet on Tag. A lot of loggers felt as Uncle Marsh did. They didn't like Tag but he could be mean and crafty and that, they argued, was what won dog fights.

Mother didn't like the way the men talked and she warned me that if ever Tag and Prince got into a fight I should come right home. I protested that everyone would be there, even Dad.

"You and I will be home," she declared with a firm mouth and a tight chin, "and so will your father." I had a feeling she hadn't yet talked to Dad but I thought it best not to say anything.

I don't know which one of the Johnson boys it was, but I think it was Jake, who got the fight started. Mr. Slater and Tag were almost to the county bridge when Jake yelled out, "Go get him, Prince."

Jake and Prince were like Tag and Mr. Slater. They adored each other. When Jake told Prince to do something he would do it. Jake's command seemed to surprise him. He stopped barking and turned to look at Jake.

"Get him," repeated Jake. That was confirmation enough. Prince bristled like a porcupine and began circling Mr. Slater and Tag, belly close to the ground and strange noises deep in his throat.

Tag got the message immediately. This wasn't the usual, bothersome Prince. Tag stopped, stiffened, and looked at Mr. Slater.

"Call off your dog," Mr. Slater shouted at Jake and Mrs. Johnson.

"Call him off yourself," smirked Jake. Mrs. Johnson didn't say anything. I walked over beside her. I wasn't certain whether I should go home or stay and see what would happen.

"Are they going to fight?" I asked Mrs. Johnson.

"Not if I can help it," she answered. She turned and gave

Jake a crack across the rear end with her broom. "Get your hinder in the house and you stay there," she ordered. "You, too," she snapped, nodding toward Fen. Both boys did as they were told. She then turned toward the county road and Mr. Slater and Tag.

"Come here, Prince," she yelled at the Johnson dog. Prince paid no attention. He was circling Mr. Slater and Tag and still making those scary, deep-throated sounds.

"Damn you, Prince, come here," shouted Mrs. Johnson. Prince, ignoring the command, circled closer and closer to Mr. Slater and Tag.

"Call off your dog or I let Tag loose," warned Mr. Slater.

"What the hell do you think I'm tryin' to do," bellowed Mrs. Johnson, meanwhile cursing and ordering Prince to no avail.

Mr. Slater bent over Tag, loosened his leash, and stepped back. In seconds the two dogs were all over each other.

"You sonofabitch," screamed Mrs. Johnson.

"I warned you," yelled back Mr. Slater.

I knew this was the dog fight Mother had warned me about. Mother's instructions had been to report home instead of watch. Camp people were beginning to gather, drawn by the noise of the fight. Uncle Marsh was there, big and assured, but I didn't see Aunt Blanche. Daddy and Ida O'Hoyt came hurrying up. Mr. and Mrs. Casey were there and so was Mr. Cox. The fight was almost in the yard of the Peets family, so they were all here. I saw my best friend Rex Gaynor and his dad. I hurried up to Uncle Marsh.

"Can I watch?" I asked timidly.

"I think you had better go home," he advised; "your mother will be looking for you." I stood transfixed for a moment watching the two dogs. There was no barking or yipping. Just exposed fangs, violent lunges punctuated by high-pitched growling sounds that made the hair on your neck stand stiff and straight. Prince had a long slash down across a front shoulder and one of his ears was nearly torn off. The blood from both dogs was beginning to color the ground where they fought. Tag was like I had never seen him before. He was cut and slashed by Prince's teeth but he kept boring in, cold, deadly, and insensitive to pain. It was as though the two dogs were fighting within an enclosure. They never seemed to move more than ten feet from where they had begun the fight.

Mrs. Johnson came hurrying up with a bucket of water and threw it on the dogs. I don't think they even noticed it.

"Can't somebody stop this?" she shouted.

"Ain't nothin' to be done," volunteered Daddy O'Hoyt. "This is a fight to the death."

I watched Mr. Slater. His face was a mask but every time his dog, Tag, would draw blood on Prince I could hear him saying things like, "Atta boy, Tag, get 'im."

Pretty soon I didn't like the fight any more. I knew an animal was going to die and that none of those gathered around, even my own Uncle Marsh, was going to care much. Suddenly the tears came and I began to cry.

"I don't want Tag or Prince to die," I shouted. "I don't want them to die." Prince was just my age—he was six.

Uncle Marsh took me by the hand. "Come," he said, "it is time we went home." His hand was big and strong. We headed toward the path through the underbrush. As we passed Mrs. Johnson I saw tears in her eyes, too. For the first time I realized she loved Prince and didn't want to see him hurt. Uncle Marsh noticed them and offered a word of comfort.

"It's been a long time coming," he said. He paused a moment, then shrugged. "It's just one of those things," he added. "Nobody's to blame, just one of those things." Mrs. Johnson nodded and started walking toward her house.

By the time we got home Mother had heard the sounds of the fight and from the number of people heading down the track and through our path in the brush suspected that Tag and Prince had finally met. Dad was outside chopping stovewood and he never stopped.

"The fight's on," said Uncle Marsh.

"I figured as much," said Dad.

Uncle Marsh let go of my hand and headed back down the path toward the fight. Dad kept right on chopping stovewood.

"Did you watch the fight?" he asked without looking up.

"A little bit," I answered. Dad, Mother, and I had a pact. It was Dad's idea. If I told the truth I would not get a licking, but if I ever lied about something and Dad found out I had lied I wouldn't be able to sit down for a week. It was a pact that we observed throughout Mother's and Dad's lives. Sometimes it was terribly embarrassing and awkward to have to tell the truth but it proved itself over and over. I grew up with a clear conscience and never during my boyhood was I afraid to go to Dad and Mother with a problem.

Camp people continued to hurry by our house headed down the tracks toward the county road and the Johnsons'. Mr. Bramble came by, as did Mr. Robinson and Jim Irving and several loggers whom I didn't know.

"Ain't you comin' to the fight, Sam?" Mr. Bramble asked Dad. Dad shook his head.

"I got work to do," he answered, swinging his double-bit ax at a chunk of fir wood. Mr. Bramble hurried on, anxious to see Prince get his "comeuppance," as Mr. Gaynor would say.

The noise of the fight seemed to grow louder and I could hear the voices of onlookers encouraging their favorites. I didn't hear Uncle Marshall's voice and I was glad about that, but I could hear Daddy O'Hoyt and Mr. Bramble urging Tag to "git 'im, Tag, go git 'im." I wondered what Mrs. Johnson and Fen and Jake would do if something happened to Prince. I wondered about Mr. Slater if Tag got hurt. It occurred to me that no matter which dog won, nothing would be settled and nobody would be really happy. I seemed to want to talk to Mother. I walked up the plank step to our porch and into the house. Mother was baking a cake in the oven, which was why she hadn't been outside. She motioned me not to slam the door or walk heavily since almost anything could shake our house and if that happened the cake would fall. I closed the door gently and tiptoed across the floor to my cot and sat down.

"Will Prince or Tag be killed?" I asked. Mother said she didn't know but she hoped not. She crossed the room and sat down on the cot beside me. She asked the same question as Dad: Had I watched the fight? I told her just a little bit.

"But I didn't like it," I sobbed, tears welling from my eyes and running down my cheeks. She dabbed at the tears with a corner of her apron.

"Sometimes animals have to fight," she said slowly. "It is nature's way of proving superiority. But God gave man a brain so that man wouldn't have to fight." I pointed out that men were fighting now, that the Western Cooperage had a lot of soldiers working as loggers to get out spruce for airplanes and stuff.

"Man isn't using his brain," she replied sadly. "When you don't use your brain you do things the hard way and get yourself into trouble. Your father and your Uncle Marsh never fight because they use their brains," she explained. I reminded her that they were big and strong and there weren't many loggers around who would pick a fight with them. Mother smiled a tiny little smile.

"It takes more character not to fight when you are big than it does when you are small," she said. That made sense. I knew that Dad could whip Mr. Bramble with one hand in his pocket but I also knew that no matter how mad he might get at Mr. Bramble he would never fight him. I suddenly felt a great surge of new pride for Dad. I was thinking about that when it dawned on Mother and me that the noise of the dog fight was gone. The Western Cooperage camp was suddenly quiet.

Mother got up from the cot, walked to the door, and opened it. People were coming up the railroad track and through the path from the Johnson house. Mr. Robinson and Mr. Irving emerged from the path. They stopped and talked with Dad a moment.

"What happened?" I heard Dad ask.

"I'd say a draw," said Mr. Robinson. "Both dogs was so plumb wore out and cut up they could hardly stand up. I ain't never seen such a fight. That Johnson dog has guts," he said with admiration in his voice. "I always figured he was a cowardly cuss. But he ain't. He's got guts." With that he and Mr. Irving moved on and Dad turned back to his wood-splitting.

The path seemed full of people, so I walked down the railroad track toward the crossing and the county road. On the way I met Mr. Slater walking slowly with Tag. Tag was covered with blood and walking real slow as though every move hurt something fierce.

I said, "Hello, Tag," but he was too tired even to wag the tip of his tail. "Will Tag be all right?" I asked Mr. Slater. Mr. Slater nodded.

"I think so," he said. I wanted to ask about Prince but I didn't. I walked down to the county road and over to the Johnsons'. Mrs. Johnson and Fen and Jake were in the yard standing around Prince. Mr. Johnson wasn't there because he cut wood for the donkey engines and sometimes worked when Dad and the others were home. Prince looked much worse than Tag. He was slashed and torn and collapsed on the ground. His eyes were shut and except for the breathing motion of his sides I would have guessed he was dead.

"Is Prince going to die?" I asked Mrs. Johnson.

"He might," she said. "He's awful sick."

"If he dies," vowed Jake, "I'll shoot that goddamn Tag and old man Slater, too."

Mrs. Johnson turned on him like a she cougar. "You'll do no such thing," she snarled. "It was you who started this fight by sicking Prince on Tag and don't you go blaming anybody else, Mr. Slater, me, or anyone." Jake was only two or three years older than me and a lot of camp people said he was just as mean as the Johnson dog, Prince. But I never found him mean. He taught me how to shoot a .22 rifle and how to set traps and gave me my first chew of tobacco (which made me terribly sick). Mother and Dad wouldn't let me set traps and catch animals and both had a horror of guns. The only thing left was to chew tobacco and after that first try I knew I didn't want to do that.

When it came to disciplining Jake and Fen, Mrs. Johnson usually used a switch or a stick. Jake was used to that but when his mother turned on him with words he was unprepared. He stared at her with a hurt look. Suddenly he began to cry and ran into the house.

Fen got down on his knees beside Prince and talked to him but Prince didn't seem to hear. He wanted to pet him but it didn't look as though there was a spot on his head or body a person could touch without hurting him.

"He ain't going to make it, Fen," Mrs. Johnson said. "He's dyin' right now. You better dig him a nice grave." With that she started to sob. It was the first time anyone, as far as I know, had seen Mrs. Johnson break down and really cry. That got Fen started and pretty soon I was crying, too. Fen and I got a shovel and I helped him dig.

"By the crick," directed Mrs. Johnson, between sobs. "Prince liked the crick."

It was kind of hard digging because by the creek there were lots of stones but we got the grave dug. We lined it with moss and fern and maple leaves so it would be soft. By the time we got the grave dug it was almost suppertime and I heard Mother calling me. I said I would come back tomorrow and see Prince and maybe he would be better and we wouldn't need the grave. Fen nodded and said he hoped so. He said his mother brought Prince home as a puppy and he had been with the Johnsons ever since. I looked for Jake but he stayed inside the Johnson tent house.

I told Mother and Dad about Prince and how Fen and I had dug a grave and lined it with moss, fern, and leaves. I thought they would be interested but neither said very much. Mother said I was a very thoughtful boy but she didn't think Prince

98

would die. But she said if he did, it was because God had need of him and wanted him in heaven. I told her Mrs. Johnson and Fen and Jake wanted him, too. How was God to know who wanted him most? And wasn't that like Dad taking something from a little person? Mother said that was why God was God. He could make those kinds of decisions. It didn't seem much of an answer but then, God was a grownup just like Mother and Dad, and grownups did funny things sometimes. Like standing around and watching dogs fight, or shooting animals. Or starting wars.

The next morning when I went over to the Johnsons' Prince wasn't in the yard. I knocked on the door and Mrs. Johnson answered.

"Where's Prince?" I asked.

"Prince is gone," she said, nodding toward the grave Fen and I had dug. I could feel tears coming and then Fen and Jake were at the door and they were crying. The three of us went over to the grave. Jake had nailed two limbs together and made a cross. It was a real nice cross and I told Jake so.

We talked about Prince and the fight and about other dogs in camp and people. I mentioned that Mother had told me that when anyone dies, dogs or people, they go to heaven. Fen and Jake were real interested and wanted to know all about heaven. I said Mother knew more about it than I did. There was silence for a while and then Jake spoke up.

"Our ma says your ma knows quite a bit about heaven. Would she tell us about it?" I said I guessed she would but there wasn't much to tell. That it was a nice place but nobody who had been there ever came back except Mr. Jesus Christ and He was there a long, long time ago and maybe things had changed there by now. Fen and Jake said that all that didn't matter. They'd like to know even a little bit about where Prince was.

We went over to our house and while Fen and Jake stood on the porch I went inside and told Mother they wanted to know about heaven where Prince was. Mother seemed a little taken aback and undecided just what to do. She finally invited Fen and Jake to come inside and have some doughnuts and milk. While we munched doughnuts and drank milk she told us about heaven. When she finished Fen and Jake said it was the nicest story they had ever heard and they weren't mad at Tag and Mr. Slater any more because Prince was in the nicest place a body could imagine and they bet even if he could come back to earth he wouldn't want to. Mother said they were probably right.

That was how our Sunday school got started. It eventually was held in the schoolhouse but the first one was held Wednesday afternoons in our house and it was for me and Fen and Jake and sometimes Mrs. Johnson.

11
When God Speaks

Most times God was pretty patient with our camp and its people but sometimes He would get irritated and scare the daylights out of us kids and sometimes our mothers.

It seemed that every time I did something wrong God knew about it and would let me know He knew about it. One time when I took a nickel from Mother's purse to buy a Hoefler Centennial chocolate from the display of candy Mr. Bramble kept in the office, the Lord sent down such a storm of thunder and lightning I confessed to Mother what I had done.

Centennial chocolates were made by Mr. and Mrs. Hoefler in Astoria and they were the finest chocolates in the whole world. Having a Centennial chocolate all to yourself was a rare treat. Fen and Jake Johnson said never in their whole life had they ever had one.

Mother said she didn't think God was angry with me and had sent the thunder and lightning storm to frighten me. She said it was my conscience that had made me confess; that the thunder and lightning storm had just been a coincidence. She said God had a lot of things to keep track of so He gave man a conscience so man could kind of keep track of himself. One Wednesday at

Sunday school Mother talked about conscience and God. Mrs. Johnson was there and she was real impressed.

She said giving man a conscience was real smart on God's part but how about people like Sharkey Bramble and that Mr. Kaiser fellow who started the war in Europe? Mother seemed a little hard pressed for an answer but she said that just because Mrs. Johnson didn't like Mr. Bramble didn't mean that Mr. Bramble was bad. Mother said the German fellow was not "Mr. Kaiser," he was just a kaiser, which was kind of like being a president. She said with people like the kaiser we would just have to trust God because God knew what He was doing.

"I still don't like the sonofabitch," declared Mrs. Johnson, "and I ain't fond of Sharkey Bramble, either."

Mother got real sharp with Mrs. Johnson and told her right out she would have to stop swearing in Sunday school.

Mrs. Johnson wanted to know why it was bad to say "Jesus Christ" if you bumped your head and not bad to say it out loud from the Bible? Mother said she had to get some pies in the oven and Sunday school was dismissed. Mrs. Johnson lit up her corncob pipe (Mother wouldn't let her smoke during Sunday school) and shuffled out the door. From the porch she turned and faced Mother.

"I may have to ease up on this Sunday school," she apologized to Mother; "they's just too goddamn many things to learn."

Mother's Sunday school information that she passed on to us came from reading the Bible and what she remembered from her own Sunday school and church days in East Boston. But as she used to tell us, that was no particular problem because God was all around in the chatter of a bluejay, the song of Klaskanine Creek, and everything from the tiny wild violets that appeared in the spring to the massive Douglas fir that towered over our heads.

She even included dogs like Prince and Tag, cats like our Muff, and nature's wild creatures such as Old Jack, an aged cougar that staked out as his territory an area between Potter and

Chester's camp and our camp. It took a little extra effort on Mother's part to include Old Jack because she was scared to death of the woods after dark and would never forget the screech owl episode her first night in camp. She still insisted it was a cougar that had been on our roof.

It was about this time that Mother began reading me stories by Thornton W. Burgess about Old Mother Nature and all her creatures such as Sammy Jay, Peter Rabbit, Jimmy Skunk, Billy Mink, Yowler the Bob Cat, Puma the Panther, Buster Bear, and all the others. Most of the creatures Mr. Burgess wrote about we had in abundance in the woods around our camp.

But where we got into trouble was distinguishing between Mother Nature and God. To my mind God was a man, maybe like Dad, a big, powerful fellow who could take a mountain and rip its top off, or throw a thunderbolt clear from heaven down to earth if He got mad.

To me Mother Nature was a plump, jolly old lady something like Mrs. Johnson, who was patient and nice most of the time but who could lay out a string of cuss words if she had to and who wasn't afraid of anything. Mrs. Johnson figured that Mother Nature was God's wife. It was quite a shock to the class when Mother told us God and Mother Nature were one and the same.

"You mean to tell me God is a woman?" gasped a stunned Mrs. Johnson. Mother said she didn't mean that at all. She said God was simply God. He was everything and everybody. He wasn't a man; and He wasn't a woman.

"You mean he's been castrated?" asked Mrs. Johnson.

"For heaven's sake, Mrs. Johnson," yelled Mother, "no, no, no. I don't mean that at all." Mrs. Johnson was on her feet.

"How come," she wanted to know, "that when you speak right out and say 'heaven' it is all right, but when I say 'hell' it is cussing?"

Mother just seemed to go to pieces.

"I'm swearing, Mrs. Johnson, dammit I'm swearing," she

shouted, "class is over. Now, will you all get out of here and go home?"

"I am home," I reminded her. "Should I go home with Mrs. Johnson?" She knelt down on the floor and swept me into her arms. Tears were running down her cheeks and she held me so tight I could hardly breathe. "I don't want any of you to go home," she sobbed. "I didn't mean what I said. I want you to stay and we'll all have hot bread with blackberry jam and milk. What do you say?"

"I'd rather have some hot bread and jam than have to learn about God," volunteered Fen. He spoke for all of us. At least for the moment.

Mother eventually worked up an explanation of God and Mother Nature that seemed to satisfy Mrs. Johnson and Fen and Jake and me. She said God was the real boss. He was in charge of everything and although Mother Nature was just another name for God we would make her a separate person for the Western Cooperage camp. She likened God to Mr. Robinson and Mother Nature to Jim Irving, the Cooperage woods boss. When God was busy, as with the big war in Europe, Mother Nature took care of things at the local level.

Mrs. Johnson wondered if God or Mother Nature would be doing anything about George Brunner down at Potter and Chester's. It seems the Potter and Chester camp was overrun with cats. Cats were a problem in many logging camps because people who had cats as pets would often leave them behind when they would move on to some other camp. The cats would eventually turn wild, breed, and have kittens that in turn were wild. Mother could work herself into a tizzy over the practice and kept insisting that people should be responsible for their pets and should take care of them.

Dad said he had never heard of a Western Cooperage cat going hungry unless it was too lazy to chew. The camp was well supplied with rats, mice, birds of all kinds, and cookhouse scraps. There were old sheds, boxes, stump shelters, and burrows by the hundreds to nest and sleep in. And there was Klaskanine Creek and rain pools by the thousands to drink from. Our own cat, Muff, lived off the land as much as she did from our table. I once saw her nail a big woods rabbit and she was always coming home with chipmunks. Sometimes she would bring them home alive just to play with. When that happened Mother would go after her with a broom. The chipmunk would escape and Muff would be furious at Mother.

The Western Cooperage seemed to get along with its cat population, owned and unowned, but at the Potter and Chester camp they got to be a real nuisance. Mr. Brunner told Dad it was almost an invasion. They were underfoot all around the cookhouse, sneaked into homes and stole food, meowed and fought all night, and sometimes would even attack young hens.

Well, Mr. Brunner offered fifty cents for every cat that was eliminated. Fen and Jake took down ten from the Western Cooperage and although Mr. Brunner was suspicious he paid them the five dollars. The orphaned cat population seemed to melt away and Fen and Jake went up to the company office and bought a whole dozen Hoefler Centennial chocolates and ate them right down like cookies.

"I never had such good eating in my whole life," marveled Fen, telling me about it later.

Mother never had to answer Mrs. Johnson's question as to what God or Mother Nature might do to Mr. Brunner about his handling of the cat problem. I guess maybe God figured Mr. Brunner had a problem and solved it the best way He could. And it did solve it, at least for a time. And when Mrs. Johnson's boys started showing up at home with one- and five-dollar bills Mrs. Johnson dropped the matter about God, cats, and Mr. Brunner. Dad said Mr. Brunner's cat elimination program cost him over one hundred dollars. Fen and Jake earned enough to buy new .22 caliber rifles in addition to daily trips to the office for Hoefler Centennial chocolates.

Mr. Brunner's plan was to reduce the cat population around

his own camp but his program reached into several camps including the California Barrel, Fischer and Leitzel, and the Western Cooperage. Some of the Western Cooperage family pets disappeared during the elimination program but our Muff survived.

One afternoon during our Sunday school session a violent thunder and lightning storm raged around the camp. A bolt of lightning struck a big hemlock across the creek from the blacksmith shop and ripped it to pieces right off the stump. Big slabs were tossed clear across the creek and one was bound tightly in telephone wire. A telephone line had been hooked to the tree. It was a terrible storm and Mother, Fen, Jake, and I were scared out of our wits and crying. Mrs. Johnson didn't seem to mind. In fact, she seemed to enjoy it.

"That's no Mother Nature storm," she shouted at Mother over the crash of thunder, "that's a God storm." Mother was sitting on my cot with Fen, Jake, and me.

After the worst of the thunder and lightning storm had passed, the wind and the rain moved in. A section of Lena Boyle's woodshed roof broke loose and came floating across the railroad track and ended in a pile of rubble on top of Mother's sweet peas. Mrs. Boyle came out on her porch for a moment and looked, then she dashed back inside. Pretty soon she came out again but this time she had her girls, Helen and Rose Mary, and her boy who was a baby. They came running across the track through the wind and rain to our house. Mother opened the door to let them in.

"Did you hear those trees coming down?" asked Mrs. Boyle. She was scared. Helen and Rose Mary started to bawl and that set off the baby and pretty soon Fen and Jake and I were at it again.

"Fer chrissake," yelled Mrs. Johnson, "will you kids shut up? There ain't nothin' goin' to happen to us. I bet God just got pissed off at George Brunner and his cats and is showin' us who's boss." She cast an eye at Fen and Jake. She shook a finger at them. "It might not hurt if you two would say that prayer Mrs. Churchill taught us." Jake began to bawl even harder and said he couldn't remember it.

"Well, goddammit say somethin'," yelled Mrs. Johnson. "Tell Him you're sorry you shot Mrs. Boyle's pet cat."

Mrs. Boyle was out of her chair as if she'd sat on a nail.

"If I didn't have this baby in my arms I'd turn you over my knee and warm your behind with a piece of stovewood," she thundered. Jake's bawling was louder than the thunder.

"I didn't shoot your cat," he screamed in terror, "Fen did it." Mrs. Boyle said it didn't matter, she'd whip them both.

During the uproar Mother had been at the kitchen stove. Now, in a quiet voice, she proposed: "What say we forget Lena's cat, the storm, and everything unpleasant? If you will all gather around the table I'll serve hot cocoa and cookies." With that she set out a cup and saucer for each of us and a big platter of cookies. I can say one thing about Mother, she was the best cookie maker in camp and she was equally good at making hot cocoa. I think part of her success was due to quantity. When she made hot cocoa she would make enough for three families, and Dad and I, after saving a cup for Mother, would drink the rest of it.

On the day of the big storm Mother's hot cocoa and cookies calmed the brewing Johnson-Boyle storm.

Long before quitting time Dad and the other men came home from the woods. Dad said the wind really raged up on the high ridges where they were logging. Big trees were crashing to earth all around them, so Mr. Robinson and Mr. Irving closed down the operation and sent the men home.

Mother and I liked having Dad home on rainy, stormy days. For one thing, it was kind of like having God right in the house with you. You knew that whatever happened Dad could take care of it. During those heavy winter rains it wasn't hard to take my afternoon nap. Mother would tuck me in under the covers, stoke up the cast-iron heating stove with big chunks of fir wood that Dad always had ready, and seat herself in front of the stove in Dad's big rocking chair. While I slept she would read. The drumming of the rain on our tar-paper roof was made to order to lull little boys to sleep. It could lull grownups, too. Sometimes on rainy days I would wake up from my nap and there would be Mother lying beside me on my cot and sound asleep.

Sometimes if I awoke early from my nap Mother would swing Dad's rocking chair around and read me a story from Mr. Burgess's *Animal Book for Children*. That was my favorite book. Mrs. Johnson liked it, too.

She came by the house one day while Mother was reading about Striped Chipmunk. We had lots of chipmunks around camp and Fen and Jake used to catch them in a box trap and make pets of them. When Mrs. Johnson came Mother stopped reading but I wanted her to finish the story.

"You've heard it a dozen times, Samuel," she told me.

"Just this one more time," I pleaded.

"Go ahead, Caroline, finish Samuel's story," Mrs. Johnson urged Mother.

Well, Mother took up the story where she had left off. Mrs. Johnson sat down on my cot and listened with me. Mother was an awful good reader. She could make you think you were really listening to Striped Chipmunk, and Mother Nature, and all the forest people that went to Mother Nature's school.

Mrs. Johnson got so interested that when Mother finished with Striped Chipmunk we talked her into reading about Johnny Chuck, and then Prickly Porky the Porcupine. We wanted her to keep on going but she said she had to stop to start supper for Dad.

Mrs. Johnson asked if she could come over again and listen while Mother read.

"Them's good stories," she declared. "Could my Fen and Jake hear them?" Mother wasn't quite ready for a daily reading session from *The Burgess Animal Book for Children* for Mrs. John-

Some of the Western Cooperage office crew (Spruce Division soldiers) in 1918. The man in the window is Sharkey Bramble, book-keeper, now dead. Standing lower left is thought to be Henry Fields, now living in Walla Walla, Washington. Others not known.

Klaskanine Creek as it is today. The old swimming hole was just to the right of the rapids, lower right.

Steam donkey loaded on logging railroad flatcar at old Western Cooperage Company camp near Olney, Oregon, and about to be hauled to new logging location. Big Sam Churchill (hatless) sitting on donkey sled directly over front wheel of car, left.

Mr. Casey's Two-Spot Shay locomotive about 1914 during early construction of Western Cooperage Company's new headquarters camp. The big building is the machine shop.

Loggers grab a precarious seating on crew train headed for the logging area. Note rain gear and calk shoes.

Typical log loading scene in the Pacific Northwest during the railroad and steam donkey era. Railroad trucks support each end of logs and are not connected except by the logs.

son, me, Fen, and Jake, but she didn't want to hurt Mrs. Johnson's feelings so she said yes.

Since she was teaching us about the Bible on Wednesday afternoons she suggested reading the Burgess book on Monday afternoons. Mrs. Johnson said that would be fine.

"I could ring Johnny Chuck's neck," Mother said to Dad that night at supper. Dad said he couldn't imagine what she was talking about. Mother told him about Mrs. Johnson and how Mrs. Johnson was all excited about Striped Chipmunk and Johnny Chuck and Mother Nature's school in Mr. Burgess's *Animal Book*.

Dad laughed so hard he blew potato all over the supper table. Mother told him not to laugh with his mouth full of food. She was always telling me not to talk when I had food in my mouth. Dad finally got his mouthful of food down and then he laughed so hard tears ran down his cheeks.

At first Mother was a little upset with him but finally even she had to smile and then she finally broke down and laughed. I couldn't for the life of me see what was so funny, but then, Dad and Mother were always laughing at things that to me weren't at all funny.

When Mother finally caught her breath she told Dad that it was no laughing matter because she was going to read to Mrs. Johnson, me, Fen, and Jake every Monday afternoon. That sent Dad into another fit of laughter. Dad said Mother was going to turn Mrs. Johnson from a happy, blasphemous renegade into a worried, educated Christian. Then Dad, with a very solemn look on his face, told Mother she was being very unfair to the rest of the people in camp. Mother wondered in what way.

Dad said maybe Daddy and Ida O'Hoyt would like to come up and hear about Johnny Chuck, Peter Rabbit, and Mother Nature's school. He then suggested Mr. and Mrs. Robinson and Mrs. Robinson's son by another marriage, "that little hellion, Bert." Dad said Sharkey Bramble could learn a lot and how come Mother hadn't asked Harry Slater, or Aunt Blanche and

Uncle Marsh, or Lena and Eddie Boyle and their kids? And how about Mike and Annie Gaynor and their boy, Rex, who was my best friend? And then there were Mr. and Mrs. Alex Carlson and the Peetses with Phil and all their other kids. And what about old man Johnson? How come Mother wasn't including him?

Mother poured a glass of Klaskanine Creek water right over the top of Dad's head and I never saw him look so surprised, ever.

"Why did you do that?" he stammered.

"Because you shouldn't make fun of Mrs. Johnson," said Mother.

Dad said Mother was right but that he didn't really mean to make fun. He said it looked so comical in his mind's eye to see me, Fen, Jake, and old Mrs. Johnson all sitting in a circle listening to Mother read about Johnny Chuck and Peter Rabbit and Old Mother Nature and her school that he just couldn't help but laugh. And I guess he meant it because he no sooner said it than he began laughing again. And then so did Mother.

When I interrupted to ask Mother if she would read me the Johnny Chuck story again, Dad laughed so hard he choked and Mother had to pound his back so he could get his breath again.

Monday afternoon when Mother started her reading session she started laughing right in the middle of Whitefoot the Wood Mouse. Mrs. Johnson asked what was so comical. Mother said it wasn't anything that was in the book. She said she just happened to remember something.

It was all she could do to get herself under control long enough to tell us:

"Please, please don't sit in a circle."

12
Ashopping We Shall Go

Mr. Welker, a pots-and-pans peddler, was an early link between Western Cooperage wives and the outside. He always wore the same ill-fitting suit, sported a walrus mustache, and drove a Model T Ford truck that moaned and groaned its way from Astoria to isolated logging camps and farm homes strung along the dirt and gravel road that wound and climbed to Jewell and on to Birkenfeld and Mist in Columbia County's Nehalem Valley.

He made the trip several times a year, often skipping some of the worst winter months when washouts, slides, and fallen trees frequently blocked what county officials called a county road.

As the Watkins man Mr. Welker handled spices, extracts, and special elixirs such as Epsom salts, castor oil, liniment, and other first aid and good health essentials. As an independent merchant he carried a line of pots and pans, soaps, cheap jewelry, combs, and sewing aids ranging from needles to thread to all shapes, sizes, and colors of buttons.

In a pinch he could be bribed to take orders for bakery bread, shoes, corsets, and other items, which orders he would fill in Astoria and deliver at a later date.

Mother was always a little distrustful of Mr. Welker. She said he had eyes that could "see through your corset."

Mr. Welker was thoroughly disliked by Daddy O'Hoyt and Daddy O'Hoyt was thoroughly disliked by Mr. Welker. Their bitterness dated back to one time when Daddy O'Hoyt was practice-driving his brand-new Chevrolet roadster and slam-banged right into the side of Mr. Welker's Model T truck.

They hit down near the crossing where the county road crossed the Western Cooperage railroad track and I was right there when it happened. Neither man was hurt but I never heard such cussing and carrying on even from Mrs. Johnson. Mr. Welker stormed from his Model T and said Daddy O'Hoyt was a blind old goat who shouldn't be allowed on a public road with a wheelbarrow, let alone an automobile.

Daddy O'Hoyt backed his Chevrolet a few feet from Mr. Welker's Model T, stopped, and apparently got confused while shifting gears. Anyway, his car suddenly lunged ahead and whammed into Mr. Welker's Ford all over again. This time the Chevrolet ripped a hole in the side of Mr. Welker's truck and there were pots and pans, Epsom salts, and buttons flying in every direction.

"You crazy old coot," screamed Mr. Welker in a terrible rage, "get out from behind that wheel before you kill someone."

By this time a crowd had begun to gather. No one seemed to be taking the accident seriously.

"Hit 'im again, he's still talkin'," Mrs. Johnson yelled at Daddy O'Hoyt while pointing toward Mr. Welker. The crowd took it up and turned it into a chant. The people didn't really mean what they were saying. They were just in a jolly mood and Daddy O'Hoyt and Mr. Welker happened, with Mrs. Johnson's help, to provide an incident to express it.

The spontaneous outburst of gaiety got Mr. Welker all confused and flustered. He fussed and sputtered and then began picking up his scattered pots and pans, buttons, and other items that had popped free of his damaged truck. Daddy O'Hoyt began helping him. Pretty soon everyone, even we kids, was gathering buttons and having great fun.

Finally, Daddy O'Hoyt slipped away for a moment, ducked into his henhouse, and emerged with two Mason jars of his best moonshine. There was a shout of joy from Mrs. Johnson and all the men but Mother and the other wives present looked a little stern and irritated. Mother didn't want me around where there was drinking, so she yelled out that anyone wanting hot cocoa and cookies could come up to our house. We hurriedly gathered up the rest of Mr. Welker's stuff and all the mothers and kids except Fen and Mrs. Johnson came up to our house.

Fen told me later he never had so much fun. He said after the Mason jars had been passed around a couple of times Mr. Welker began to sing and Daddy O'Hoyt and Mrs. Johnson did some kind of an Irish jig that Daddy O'Hoyt had learned as a kid from his father.

I think that was the start of Daddy O'Hoyt's troubles with Mr. Tichenor, the deputy federal marshal in Astoria, who was always hunting for moonshiners. He probably heard about the Western Cooperage crossing party and how Daddy O'Hoyt had moonshine in his chicken house. Mother said if that was what happened it served him right. Mother was sometimes hard to understand. She would never refuse to drink a glass of Daddy O'Hoyt's dandelion or elderberry wine but then she'd turn right around and say it was wrong for Daddy O'Hoyt to make it.

I asked Mrs. Johnson about that. She didn't know either but said maybe that was the way they did things in Boston. She said it was like everybody saying "Amen" when you said "God" inside a church and giving you hell when you said "God" outside, on the steps.

Another link with the outside world for Western Cooperage folks was Mr. Billy Deeds, who drove the mail truck that now carried the mail between Astoria and Jewell. Mr. Deeds was a good drinker and a jolly fellow and Mother adored him. He was younger than Daddy O'Hoyt but quite a bit older than Dad.

Although his main responsibility was getting the mail from Astoria to Jewell and to the various logging camps and farm homes in between, he also distributed the latest news and gossip. Mr. Deeds always seemed to know who was pregnant, when a logging camp was going to shut down, and when it was going to start up. He seemed to know everything.

In fact, it was Mr. Deeds who told Mother and the others at the Western Cooperage camp that the United States had declared war on Germany and we were in World War I. Mother thought he must be mistaken but when Mr. Deeds brought our newspapers they proved he was right.

Although Mr. Deeds's specialties were the mail, news, and gossip, he could be imposed upon to run errands when he was in Astoria. Fresh mail came every other day. Mr. Deeds came out from Astoria with the mail one day and would return with the outgoing mail the next day. Sometimes in winter when fallen trees, washouts, or slides blocked the road the mail would come by boat or truck to Olney and then up to our camp by log train.

Mr. Deeds was always impressed by the number of books, magazines, letters, and other stuff Mother got in the mail. He said Mother's mail took up more room in the Western Cooperage mail pouch than all the rest of the camp put together. Mother said that was because she wrote a lot of letters and liked reading books and magazines.

One time Mr. Deeds told me that if I knew just half of what Mother did I wouldn't have to go to school. I asked Mother about that because it was spring and I was getting tired of school and half of something didn't seem like very much. Mother gave Mr. Deeds a bad look and told me that no matter how much a body knew he should go to school.

One of the best places to visit in the whole world, at least for me, was Mrs. Olson's Olney Hotel and general store. For one thing, going to Olney meant a ride with Mr. Casey and Oscar Ward on Shay locomotive No. 2. For another thing, Mrs. Olson could always be depended upon to know precisely what pleased a small boy's stomach. Invariably it was hot bread with fresh butter and sugar, big fat sugar cookies or doughnuts, and fresh milk.

Mrs. Olson's store was something else. It carried everything from ladies' hairpins to horse collars and in between there were candies, dress goods, groceries, toys, rain gear, and crosscut saws.

Mother loved to poke around the crowded aisles and showcases of Mrs. Olson's store. She would admire dress goods and clothing by the hour and stroke laces and other materials as though they were warm, living things. Mother loved style and quality and although Mrs. Olson's store was no Boston salon it was a big step from the logging camp world of baggy house dresses, calk shoes, black wool underwear, and hard-weaved hickory shirts that could fend off brush, thorns, and a fair amount of moisture.

Mrs. Olson's Olney with its hotel, store, blacksmith shop, dock, warehouse, and heavy plank sidewalks on each side of the road was a bustling farm and logging community. It was quite a contrast to the Western Cooperage camp with its cramped little commissary, railroad track, and footpaths. At Olney you could ride a tricycle or play with a coaster wagon on the plank sidewalks. At the Western Cooperage there was no place for either. There was no place to bat a ball without losing it in the brush.

The Western Cooperage was missing a lot of things but, as Mother used to point out, maybe we didn't have a nice park like ones in a city but we had a thousand square miles of forest, mountains, and meadows; we didn't have a church but we had God; we didn't have a zoo but we had more animals and birds than you would ever see in a zoo and we had them free and uninhibited right at our doorstep.

We didn't have a lot of things city kids had, including child molesters, burglaries, and holdups.

We didn't have a big, fancy school. But we had a teacher who loved us. We didn't have electricity or street lights but we had a vast dome of a sky that on summer nights opened up billions of tiny stars that twinkled and glowed and showered peace and quiet and contentment down upon us.

"Samuel is growing up in a vacuum," my Aunt Sue Frates, who came out from the East to visit Mother one summer, remarked.

"A vacuum?" Mother stared at her sister in wonder. "Are you telling me that growing up with God on your doorstep is growing up in a vacuum?"

Mother and Aunt Sue were awfully close but they did like to argue. Now, my cousins Carol and Bill Frates liked our camp. They said it was a lot better than Boston, Miami, and some of the other places they had lived. They loved riding in the cab of little No. 2 Shay with Mr. Casey, or playing in the machine shop, or watching Dad at work in the woods with the big steam donkey engines whistling, roaring, and straining.

Olney was a nice place to visit but Mother and I were always happy to get back to our camp, home, and Dad.

Next to Mrs. Olson's Olney my favorite shopping spot was the Columbia River town of Astoria.

Founded by John Jacob Astor's Pacific Fur Company in 1811 as a fur trading post, it outgrew its pioneer origins, and by the time Dad and Mother knew it, it had matured into a civilized sin city built on piling. It was a city of planked streets, big timber, and salmon. Lewis and Clark paddled by it and spent the winter of 1805–6 camped only a half-dozen miles from it. The site of the old Pacific Fur Company's Fort Astoria was just across the street from the hospital where I was born.

But by that time Astorians wouldn't have known a beaver pelt from a skunk hide, they were so enmeshed in fish, fun, and lumber. More than half of Astoria's population was Scandinavian.

Mother said that in 1911, the year I was born, Astoria had fifty-two saloons and twelve churches. The shores of the Columbia River were lined with sawmills and fish canneries. There were only a half-dozen Smiths in the business directory, but 127 Johnsons. Dad said Astoria had more Swedes than Sweden.

Despite its hills, rain, planked streets, and brothels, Mother loved Astoria. She said it reminded her of Boston because both had played such important parts in the history of the United States. Boston was kind of a pivot and inspiration for freedom; Astoria was the pivot upon which the United States laid claim to 745 miles of the Columbia River, from its mouth to the present border of Canada. In addition to that it was one hundred years old the year I was born.

Astoria was a city of wind and tide. It prospered in direct proportion to its gifts from the river and the sea and from the boundless forests that cloaked its hinterlands. When Mother stepped from the train at the Astoria depot in 1911 those forests, by government estimate, totaled some 15 billion board feet in Clatsop County alone. Another 60 billion were within reach of Astoria as a trading area.

It was easy to understand why Dad and so many loggers of his day could see no way in the foreseeable future that man could fall, yard, and transport all that forest to sawmills. But he did. And he did it in the unbelievably short span of ninety-nine years from 1843, when a Mr. Henry H. Hunt put up the first crude water-powered sawmill in Clatsop County some twenty miles or so upriver from Astoria, to 1942, when Tidewater Timber Company, the successor to the old Western Cooperage Company, hauled its last log over what was left of the old Western Cooperage Company railroad.

To my father and to my Uncle Marsh, and to tens of thousands of others just like them, it was incredible. A thousand square miles of forest, gone!

But to a small boy in 1918 the sound and the fury, the noise and the optimism were still there. Astoria, in its own peculiar way, symbolized everything I believed in—Mother and Dad, God, trees, the sea, and the river. They were there when I needed them as a boy; they would be there when I would need them again, as a man. They symbolized strength, permanence, and stability.

To my mind Astoria was just about the biggest, busiest place a body could imagine. My favorite retail store was Foard and Stokes, an emporium so diverse in its offerings it advertised everything from Haviland china to steam donkey engines. You could wander its aisles for days and never see the same item twice. Mother said it was almost as good as going to a museum.

A shopping trip from the camp to Astoria was generally a two-day trip since it took most of one day just to go back and forth. When in Astoria Mother usually stayed at the Weinhard-Astoria Hotel, a four-story brick hostelry with elevators, bathtubs, and a dining room where waiters brought you ice water in long-stemmed goblets. The finest dinner, served on a linen tablecloth and with linen napkins to wipe your mouth and keep food spots off your clothes, was seventy-five cents.

Mother was proud of the Weinhard-Astoria. She said that for elegance and decor it was hard to beat, even in Boston or Portland.

Invariably our shopping trips to Astoria included lessons in history and manners. Sometimes we would visit the site of Mr. Astor's old Fort Astoria. Part of the site was on an old vacant lot covered with brush and weeds. We sometimes tramped around. Mother said when we did that we left our footprints right there with those early Astorians. She said wherever you stepped you left your mark and it would be there forever and ever, even though your eye couldn't see it.

She said Dad's footprints would always be a part of the Western Cooperage woods, and hers and mine would always be in the land we walked at camp. That was pretty hard for me to believe, but if Mother said it, it had to be so. Mother knew an awful lot of things. It was she who told me that those first Astorians planted 12 potatoes in the spring and in the fall harvested 190. That was a lot better than Dad did with his potatoes at camp but Mother said it would be better if I didn't ask him about it.

There was one thing I didn't like about coming to Astoria and that was driving by the Clatsop County poor farm. It was a dull-colored stone building that sat on a rise of land right by the county road. It always looked bleak and glum and sad.

Mother said it was all of those things because it was a place that old people went when there was no one left to love or take care of them. I told Mother I didn't want to get old, that I didn't want to go to the poor farm, that it scared me.

I wondered if we, or anybody we knew, would go to the poorhouse. She said she didn't think so. She said we had each other, and so did all of our friends, and we had love and we had God, and if you had all of those things you most likely wouldn't go to the poor farm. But if something happened that you did go there, you should have faith in God, try and make someone around you happy, and then you would be happy.

One time when Mother and I were talking, she suggested we say a little prayer for all the old people in poor farms all over the world.

We did, and I felt better.

13

Sawmills and Roses

About once a year, sometimes twice, Mother and I would ride to Astoria with Billy Deeds and his mail truck and take the boat or train to Portland.

Portland, the biggest city in Oregon, was a hundred miles upriver from Astoria on the banks of the Willamette River not far from where that river joined the Columbia.

Portland was one of Mother's favorite cities, mostly, I think, because it almost was named Boston. Mother said the two founders, a Mr. A. L. Lovejoy and a Mr. Francis Pettygrove, couldn't decide whether to call it Portland, in honor of Mr. Pettygrove's favorite city in Maine, or Boston, after Mr. Lovejoy's home city in Massachusetts.

They flipped a coin and Mr. Pettygrove won, so what was to become a city of sawmills and rose gardens became Portland.

The story of Portland and how it got its name always intrigued me and I used to ask Mother to tell it to me over and over because it reminded me of Mrs. Johnson beating Sharkey Bramble out of a beef roast with a crooked coin. I couldn't help but wonder if Mr. Pettygrove used one of Fen Johnson's coins with no heads and two tails. Mother said she didn't think so because Mr. Pettygrove and Mr. Lovejoy did their coin flipping long before Fen, or even Mrs. Johnson, was born.

The thing I liked best about going to Portland was the ride on a steamboat up the Columbia and Willamette rivers or going by train.

When going by steamboat we sometimes took the night boat from Astoria. It was the *Lurline* and had a big paddle wheel at the stern that churned the river like anything. The *Lurline* had staterooms, and when Mother would tuck me in my bunk I would lie there and listen to the paddle wheel churning and churning, far into the night.

If we stayed overnight in Astoria we usually took the day boat, a trim, handsome propeller craft named the *Georgiana.* The *Georgiana* was built especially for passengers whereas the *Lurline* was designed to haul freight. On either boat the fare to Portland was one dollar.

Once in Portland I hardly ever let go of Mother's hand and when I did it was only when she was at a store counter and needed both hands to look at merchandise. Even then I held on to her skirt. Mother told me to do that. There were just so many people in Portland that walking among them on a sidewalk was like going down a Western Cooperage woods path surrounded by trees.

Mother always timed at least one of our Portland trips so it came two or three weeks before Christmas. I remember the first time. I couldn't believe there were so many Santa Clauses.

Mother explained that they were all helpers and that the real Santa was up at the North Pole getting his reindeer and sleigh ready for his Christmas trip and filling his big toy bag with names and gifts that his helpers in stores sent him.

I was always a little uneasy as Christmas drew near for fear Santa would fly right over our camp and never know we were there. After being in Portland you just wondered how he could ever find a tiny little spot like the Western Cooperage camp, hidden in Klaskanine Creek canyon deep in the Coast Range mountains where there weren't any stores and no Santa Claus helpers.

Mother always assured me there was no need to worry. She said God and Santa Claus were friends and that God knew where every single living thing, plant or animal, lived and He helped Santa. With God giving Santa a hand I felt a lot better but it was always a relief to wake up Christmas morning and see a pile of presents under the Christmas tree.

There was also the thing about no fireplace chimneys of any kind in camp. A lot of us kids were kind of uneasy about that, but all the mothers and dads left their house doors unlocked so Santa could just walk in. Mother said that was a lot easier for him than climbing down a sooty old fireplace chimney.

When I got a little older the things I wanted were an electric train and a tricycle. In my letters to Santa and on my trips to Astoria and Portland when I would see Santa's store helpers, those were what I always asked for. But on Christmas morning they were never there.

Mother finally got around to explaining that to me. She said Santa had been to the Western Cooperage camp so many times since the camp was built that he knew as much about it as I did. She said he knew we didn't have electricity in the camp or sidewalks or streets. Since I couldn't have played with an electric train or a tricycle if he brought them he gave them to some little boy who lived in a city and could use them, and gave me something a logging camp boy could use—a grown-up pocket knife, or a pocket watch that really kept time; or an air rifle to shoot at targets with; lots of good storybooks that Mother could read to me; and maybe a real steam engine that used wood alcohol to heat its water.

When you understood why Santa did certain things it helped make Christmas more fun. And anyway, I would rather have a real, live steam engine that puffed and whistled than an old electric train that wouldn't run.

But speaking of trains. Every time we were in Portland

Mother always took me down to the Union Station to watch the trains. We would stand on the Broadway Bridge where we could look right down on the station, the tracks, and all the people. It was hard to imagine so many trains and cars as they had at Portland's Union Station.

The Union Station was where Mother and Dad got off the train when they came West from Boston. I think she liked to go there partly for me and partly for herself. I think looking at the trains and people took her back in her own mind to Boston, her friends back there, and Grandma Snow, who died two years after I was born.

I know that Mother loved me and she loved Dad, and I heard her say many times how much she loved Oregon and its beautiful forests, creeks, mountains, and rivers. And she loved our camp and its people, even Mrs. Johnson.

I knew how she felt because I loved them, too. And so did Dad. But I guess if you have lived a long time in other places you sometimes think about them, too, no matter where you are or how happy you are. And when those times come you are maybe like the geese that fly North over our camp in the spring and back South in the fall—you would like to go back to where that place is and have a look, maybe for just a day, or maybe only an hour. I think that is maybe the way Mother sometimes felt when we would stand on the Broadway Bridge in Portland and look down on the trains and the Union Station.

Other than the toy departments, the stores in Portland were dull and not much fun. Mother could waste hours in places like Meier & Frank or Olds, Wortman & King, just looking and admiring. To me they weren't half as interesting as the hardware section at Foard and Stokes in Astoria or Mrs. Olson's general store at Olney. But there was something about them that seemed to please and excite Mother.

One thing I did like was staying at the Portland Hotel in Portland. It went up higher than a full-grown Douglas fir tree and one time Mother got us a room right on the top floor. We could look out our window and see half the city of Portland. I used to like to flush the toilet and listen to the water go down but Mother made me stop. She said it might bother the people in the room below us. And that brought up the question of toilets and bathtubs. Where did all the water and other stuff go?

Mother said we should talk about something else.

One of the things we did talk a lot about when in Portland was manners. Mother was a stickler for manners. At camp she insisted I be neat and clean and in Astoria or Portland she was even more fussy. I don't mean she frowned at playing outside in the rain and mud of winter, or helping Mr. Casey around those greasy and oily spots on little Shay No. 2, or playing in the machine shop where dirt and grease and dust were on everything.

She didn't fuss much about those things but she got real finicky when it came time to go to school, or company would drop in, or we would go to Olney, or Astoria, or Portland. At school I was the only boy who wore knickers that buttoned below the knee and hung down like a girl's bloomers. All the other boys wore overalls. When I was in the third grade Mother relented a bit and permitted me to let the knickers hang loose on my legs so they didn't fold over like bloomers.

The worst, I guess, was that I had to wear underwear, even in summer when it was hot and all the other kids just wore their overalls and shirts next to their bare skin.

Even at camp she taught me to open doors and let women go in or out of a place first. It always seemed to me that the one who got to the door first ought to go in or out first. But it didn't work that way with Mother. She said women should always be first. When we were walking on a sidewalk in Astoria or Portland she said the man should always walk on the side nearer the street. There were rules for going up and down stairways, washing your hands clear up past your elbows, combing your hair, and things like that. One other thing Mother couldn't stand was long or dirty fingernails. To outsiders like Fen and Jake Johnson, or Phil Peets, Mother's manner rules were worse than going to school and learning reading, writing, and arithmetic. But after you had lived with her for a while and got the hang of things it wasn't so bad. Things like opening doors and combing your hair you got so you did without even thinking about them.

Mother said that was the way they should be. Just like swallowing soup, automatic.

I used to wonder if Dad knew and did all those things. Mother said he did.

Living with Mother could at times be difficult, but when we would go to Portland and eat in a hotel or restaurant, or ride on a boat or take the train, I was always proud of her. She knew how to do so many things such as buying tickets, ordering meals, and yelling for taxis. She knew how to beckon for a redcap in the train depot, how to talk with the purser on a river boat, or how much of a tip to give a bellhop.

Being with Mother in the city was like being with Dad in the woods. People respected them, listened when they said something, and jumped when they gave an order.

I guess maybe the best part of those trips to Portland was coming back to the Western Cooperage camp and telling the other kids what I'd done and seen.

Fen and Jake Johnson had never been to Portland and when I would tell them about buildings there that could hold more people than lived in the whole Western Cooperage headquarters camp they were skeptical. In fact, Jake said I was a goddamn liar.

Well, I wasn't and Mae Casey, who had been to Portland, said I wasn't. And so did Miss Violet Olson, my third grade teacher. When I told Mother what had happened she said that sometime on one of our trips to Portland we should take Fen and Jake. When she mentioned that to Dad he said some terrible bad words but what they added up to was "No." He said he wasn't worried about Mother and me, it was just that Portland wasn't ready yet for the likes of Fen and Jake.

I guess maybe Dad was right because Mother never did ask Fen and Jake if they would like to go.

The Johnsons were awful hard to tell things to. When I told Mrs. Johnson about all the silverware they put on the table in Portland hotel dining rooms she said that was a lot of damn tomfoolery. She wanted to know what was the harm in eating your pie with the same fork you used in eating your salad, meat, and potato? I didn't know.

"They ain't one bit of harm," she challenged. "All those other forks and things are just to make more work for the people who have to wash the dishes," she said. Mrs. Johnson had some funny ideas about big companies and the people who worked for them. She said Sharkey Bramble was typical of a company man. She said her husband, Mr. Johnson, didn't work as hard as he could just so he could make up for some of the extra money the company got in the commissary from Mr. Bramble weighing his thumb.

Dad's answer to that was that Mr. Johnson was kind of a likable fellow but when it came to work he long ago was way ahead of the company and Mr. Bramble's thumb.

Before I forget it. There was one other thing about Portland that Mother adored. The people there grew thousands and thousands of roses. Mother called it the city of sawmills and roses.

Mother loved roses.

Aunt Minnie told Dad about that so that night in Boston when he gave Mother her engagement ring he also gave her a dozen roses.

Mother pressed a petal from each of the dozen roses and put them in her memory book.

Women sometimes do funny things.

Even grown-up women, like Mother.

14
Come and Get It

One of the first things most everyone at the Western Cooperage camp did when going to town was load up on ice cream. Mother's favorite was vanilla served in an ice cream soda. My specialty was a chocolate milk shake or a couple of vanilla scoops buried under a ladleful of chocolate syrup and topped with a handful of ground nuts. Aunt Blanche joined with Mother in preferring sodas.

Dad and Uncle Marshall adored ice cream. Mother said that one time before she and Dad were married he and Uncle Marsh walked from the camp to Astoria and back one Sunday just to satisfy a craving for ice cream. That was at the first Western Cooperage camp where Mother came as a bride and it was about eight miles closer to Astoria than the new headquarters camp where we now lived, but even so it was a round-trip hike of almost twenty-five miles. I asked Dad if he really did do that and he said he did. What's more, he said it was worth every step.

I guess the reason it was worth every step was that when Dad and Uncle Marsh sat down to a feed of ice cream they could easily clean up a gallon between them. It used to embarrass Mother and Aunt Blanche to go with them into an ice cream parlor or soda fountain place. They wouldn't have a thing to do with the fancy little serving dishes in such places.

"Just bring me a bowl, a big bowl," Dad used to say, smiling at the waitress. Uncle Marsh would say the same. They both loved vanilla. And when they ordered a bowl they didn't mean a small bowl like one you serve soup in; they wanted a really big bowl like the one Mrs. Olson served mashed potatoes in at her Olney Hotel.

Sometimes Dad would pour a little chocolate syrup over his heaped-up bowl. That really upset Mother. She said it made her ill to look at it. Dad used to grin and reply that she was just envious, that she would love to have a heaping bowl of ice cream, too, but she and Aunt Blanche were squeezed up so tight in their corsets there was only room enough left for a few mouthfuls in their stomachs.

That used to really set Mother's eyes to flashing because she felt mention of ladies' undergarments was not proper conversation in front of me and particularly in a public place while eating. I never said anything but I was sure Dad was right because I used to watch him cinch up Mother's corset sometimes, and believe you me, Mother wanted it tight.

There was no ice or refrigeration of any kind at the Western Cooperage camp, so ice cream was rare. We never had it during the warm summer months and only once in a while in winter.

Those winter ice cream treats were provided by Mr. and Mrs. Wilson, who were the camp cooks and had quarters in the cookhouse. Sometimes, usually in January when it got cold enough to freeze and there was snow on the ground, Mrs. Wilson would make homemade ice cream and invite us up to help make it and share in the eating.

Dad and Uncle Marsh would look forward to an early freeze in hopes Mrs. Wilson would make ice cream. She used heavy, rich cream that she skimmed from the tops of the milk cans and added to that vanilla flavoring, sugar, eggs, and maybe some other things I don't remember. For a freezer she used a big, empty lard pail nestled in a copper wash boiler filled with chunk ice from nearby ponds and packed tight with snow. Dad, Uncle Marsh, and Mr. Wilson took turns doing the churning with strong wooden paddle-like spoons. Even when the mixture started thickening, Dad and Uncle Marsh were so eager and so strong they would make that paddle fairly fly.

When it was ready to eat, Mrs. Wilson would bring out two big cookhouse bowls for Dad and Uncle Marsh, a smaller one for Mr. Wilson, who was a rather small man and couldn't eat much, and sauce dishes for me, Mother, Aunt Blanche, and herself. We would huddle close to the warmth of the cookhouse's huge wood-burning range and eat up all of Mrs. Wilson's ice cream.

Mrs. Wilson said it always pleased her to watch Dad and Uncle Marsh eat her ice cream. She said it made the effort seem more worthwhile. Mother and Aunt Blanche kept predicting that one day they would eat themselves into being sick. But they never did. The cookhouse with its myriad of good odors was one of my favorite spots and a place where a small boy could get a handout.

The camp cookhouse was the most important building in the camp. More important, even, than the office or the machine shop because the one thing an average logger demanded was good food and plenty of it. He would work in the mud, rain, summer heat and dust, risk life and limb a dozen times a day, do without company showers, sleep in drafty bunkhouses, all with a minimum of grumbling. But start cutting back on the quality and quantity of cookhouse meals and he would quit immediately and spread bad words about that camp's food wherever he went.

Since the nearest restaurant was twenty miles distant in Astoria and the nearest hotel dining room was at Mrs. Olson's hotel in Olney, ten miles by log train or a jolting road trip by car, Dad used to take us up to the cookhouse now and then for a meal out.

No matter what day it was, the evening meal at any logging

camp cookhouse was almost like Thanksgiving. There were always two or three kinds of meat, boiled or mashed potatoes, several vegetables, homemade bread, fresh milk or coffee, and for dessert a choice of two or three kinds of pie as well as cake. Most camps had women waitresses, and as soon as a platter or bowl was empty it was replaced with a full one. You could eat all you wanted and even load up for a snack later on. The dinnerware was heavy white crockery that weighed almost as much as a pair of calk shoes. You could drop a plate on the wooden floor of the cookhouse and it would just bounce.

One of the strange things about a logging camp cookhouse at mealtime, and a thing Mother could never get used to, was the silence. The only sounds were the footsteps of the waitresses, the rattle of knives and forks, and requests to pass things. Loggers just never talked while eating. To Mother, mealtime, especially the evening meal, was a time of relaxation, conversation, and laughter. In a logging camp, when a logger went to the cookhouse at mealtime he went there to eat. He could talk later in the bunkhouse. It was sort of an unwritten rule, handed down by Paul Bunyan, I guess, that when you sat down to eat you ate. Dad said it was probably because the cookhouse staff was always pushed for time and the faster the men would eat and get out the quicker the staff could get the tables cleared, dishes washed, and the tables set for the next meal. A logger rarely spent more than fifteen or twenty minutes at the cookhouse table. Mother said it was a crime to gulp down such delicious food. Dad used to tell her she had better hurry up or a waitress would clear her plate and scrub the oilcloth table covering right in front of her. They never did that but they did encourage a body to eat plenty, but eat fast.

Sunday dinner at the Western Cooperage cookhouse was memorable. It was usually chicken and dumplings with spuds and rich gravy and sometimes dressing on the side. Loggers always demanded potatoes whether or not there was also dressing or dumplings. On Sundays the cooks went all out for desserts, with big two-inch-thick pumpkin, mincemeat, or cream pies and usually a big fat chocolate and vanilla layer cake assortment. I tell you there wasn't a Portland or Astoria hotel dining room or restaurant that could match the Western Cooperage cookhouse on Sunday.

Most logging camp cookhouses of that period weren't much to look at, but once you smelled the rich odors and saw the heaping platters of food spread along the tops of the long wooden tables you forgot all about looks. A cookhouse didn't have chairs as in hotel dining rooms and restaurants. You sat on wood benches set end to end on each side of the tables. Each eating spot had a number and if you were a regular eater at the cookhouse you ate at your assigned spot and no other. When we would go up there to eat Mr. Wilson would tell us what numbers to sit at and that was where we would sit.

Dad's love for ice cream and the sparkle in his eye when we got a winter invitation to join the Wilsons in an ice cream party set Mother to thinking. Ice cream was a treat, even in winter, I heard her tell Dad, but summer was when ice cream really tasted the best. Dad said he agreed with that but what was she getting at?

Mother replied that she was trying to figure out a way we could have ice cream at the camp in summer. Dad said there was no way. Mother said there had to be a way. Dad said she could order it shipped out from a creamery in Astoria, maybe, but it would be soup before Billy Deeds, whose truck would have to deliver it, got halfway to Olney.

The next time we were in Astoria Mother checked with a creamery. The creamery people said the long trip to camp was no problem. The metal ice cream containers could be packed in ice in insulated canvas bags made for the purpose. They said the only risk would be that Billy Deeds might get hungry and eat it. But Mother said that was less of a risk than shipping a bottle of booze because then, almost for sure, Billy Deeds would drink it.

The creamery man laughed and said Mother sure enough must know Billy Deeds.

Mother made arrangements with the creamery and Billy Deeds for the delivery of twenty gallons of vanilla ice cream to our house July 3. That was Mr. Deeds's regular mail trip day from Astoria to Jewell and he could bring out the ice cream with the mail. Mother said she wanted to have an ice cream party on the Fourth of July. The creamery man assured her the insulated canvas bags and ice would keep it firm.

When Mother told Dad what she had done he was worse than I am just before Christmas. He said he wished the Fourth of July were tomorrow instead of almost a month away.

There was one little thing Mother neglected to mention to Dad. She neglected to mention that she had ordered twenty gallons and to offset the cost and maybe produce a little profit she was going to sell ice cream to the camp families. She didn't tell Dad these things because Dad had a horror of debt and was dead set against selling anything to a friend or neighbor.

"If he's a friend and you can't give it to him, then keep it," he used to say.

The creamery and Mr. Deeds did as they had promised. A little after noon on July 3 Mr. Deeds's big old Mack truck with hard rubber tires and chain drive chugged into camp and Mother's ice cream was aboard. The noon log train had gone through, so the tracks were clear. We got a section crew's push car from a siding, took it down to the county road crossing, and loaded the heavy canvas bags of ice cream and ice on that. Then with my help Mr. Deeds and Mother pushed the little push car up the track to in front of our house. We carried the bags into a little fruit room Dad had built between our house and the woodshed. It was cool in there, and as I found out later, Mother wasn't too anxious for Dad to see the amount of ice cream she had bought. As we were unloading the last bag from the push car Phil Peets and the Johnson boys happened by. They wanted to know what was in the bags. Mother told them it would be a

A logging camp cookhouse similar to the one at the Western Cooperage camp. This one would seat 450 men.

The tiny building in the center was the Western Cooperage school and teacher's house in 1915. The teacher used a blanket strung on a wire to screen her kitchen quarters from the classroom. A corner of the Churchill home is just visible at left. (*Photo courtesy of Mrs. George W. Brunner*)

Architecture in wood. One of thousands of logging railroad trestles that loggers built.

Typical logging camp of early 1920s and 1930s in Oregon and Washington. All but the building in the center are mounted on railroad
trucks so the camp could be moved by locomotives to new areas close
to the timber. (*Sam Churchill Photo*)

Caroline Snow Churchill in Boston in 1910.

secret until tomorrow. I didn't know it but she had already told the other wives in camp so they could have their cash ready for the big Fourth of July ice cream festival and sale.

Dad did just as Mother anticipated. Mother hadn't mentioned ice cream once and she cautioned me not to mention it either since the day a month previous when she had ordered it. Dad had plumb forgotten all about it. But I hadn't. All that night I tossed and twisted on my cot and had bad dreams about Fen and Jake Johnson and Phil Peets getting into our fruit house and eating all of our ice cream.

The Fourth of July was one of the biggest holidays of the year in logging camps, so most of the single men were in town celebrating and most of the married men were at home chopping wood, gardening, or doing other chores.

Mother had told the other wives that she would start selling the ice cream at one o'clock but most of them couldn't wait. We hadn't even finished lunch when people began lining up in front of our house with bowls, pots, tin buckets, and spoons.

"What in tarnation are all those people waiting for?" Dad wanted to know.

"Ice cream," answered Mother.

"Ice cream?" Dad looked at Mother in astonishment. Then he remembered. "Ice cream!" he shouted. "I forgot all about that."

He looked again at the growing line of people and then back at Mother. "How much did you buy?" he wanted to know. Mother admitted she had bought twenty gallons.

"Twenty gallons!" Dad almost fainted. But there was no time for that. The people were getting impatient, so we hurried to the fruit room and Dad brought out the big canvas bags and Mother began filling orders. Dad still thought she was simply sharing our good fortune but by the time he discovered the truth it was too late to do anything without making a scene. The tip-off was Mrs. Johnson. She had two big bowls and was the first one in line.

"Give me a heaping two dollars' worth," she told Mother.

Right behind Mrs. Johnson was Mr. Slater, who bought a dollar's worth all for himself. Even Mr. Bramble was there and so were Uncle Marsh and Aunt Blanche.

Mother's ice cream venture was a smashing success and in no time the twenty gallons were gone. She had just emptied the last scoopful into Mrs. Robinson's saucer when she looked as though she had been shot.

"Merciful God in heaven," she breathed with an expression of shock on her face, "I forgot."

"Forgot what?" asked Dad.

"Forgot to save any ice cream for us," said Mother.

"Jesus Christ," roared Dad. The soup bowl he had just picked up fell from his hands and thumped on the floor. It was about the first time I had ever heard Dad take the Lord's name in vain and I was as startled as Mother.

"Sam." Mother scowled.

Dad was so upset he began giving Mother the dickens for charging people for the ice cream. That reminded me that I wasn't going to get any and I began to cry. Mother began to cry. And Dad used those bad words again.

The Johnsons were sitting in the shade of our woodshed eating their bowls of ice cream. They couldn't help but hear what was going on.

Mrs. Johnson came over and told me not to cry. "Fen," she yelled, "bring the rest of that ice cream over here." Fen came, but dragging his feet and spooning ice cream into his mouth all the way. He had about cleaned out the bowl when Mrs. Johnson handed it to me.

"It ain't much but eat it," she ordered.

"How come he gets to eat our ice cream?" protested Fen, trying to get his spoon back.

"None of your damn business," snapped Mrs. Johnson, telling him to "go back and sit with your dad and brother."

Dad's reaction to the ice cream sales venture discouraged Mother from bringing in any more, even for giveaway, and even though people kept asking her to and to charge whatever she wanted.

Mrs. Johnson told Dad he was a pigheaded old cuss spoiling everyone's fun.

That winter Mr. and Mrs. Wilson had us up a couple of times for homemade ice cream.

I told Dad that Mother's shipped out from Astoria tasted better.

Dad said he wouldn't know since he didn't get even one spoonful of the ice cream from Astoria. He could be pigheaded.

15

Bear Meat and Watercress

Menus at the Western Cooperage camp relied to quite an extent on natural foods when those foods were in season, except for deer, which were fair game at any time a logger happened to meet up with one.

Logging camp fathers killed for the table and not for fun, so man-made game laws were simply ignored. Mrs. Johnson expressed the sentiments of most families in camp.

"Them fellers who make them game laws ain't never put any meat on our table," she told Mother, "so when we need venison we go get it."

Dad didn't hunt but if he had wanted to I doubt that Mother would have let him. She just couldn't understand how a grown man with a gun could kill any living creature, particularly a deer.

"It's murder in cold blood," she used to tell Dad.

Dad agreed in part but he was also inclined to believe that what God provided, man should use. Mother had read me so many Thornton W. Burgess bedtime stories about Lightfoot the Deer, Buster Bear, and Old Mother Nature and Peter Rabbit that venison and bear meat never tasted all that good to me.

Dad was a kind and generous man with plenty of compassion

for Mother Nature and her brood but he was also a realist who classified birds and animals in a category with trees.

"God put them here for us to use," he used to try and convince Mother, "so we should use them." Mother, despite all of Dad's logical arguments, could never bring herself to eat venison. When folks would bring over venison for Dad she would cook it but that was as far as she would go. For a long time it didn't make much difference because she couldn't tell one kind of meat from another anyway.

One day while preparing what she thought was a venison roast she told Aunt Blanche that "I couldn't eat a piece of this venison if I were starving."

Aunt Blanche told her she didn't have to worry because what she had in the roasting pan wasn't venison—it was bear meat.

Deer kills by cougar were plentiful around the camp in winter and that disturbed Mother. She said God was a little unfair when he let Buster Bear sleep, safe and sound, much of the winter and made Lightfoot the Deer forage for food in wind and snow while trying to outwit man and his gun and cougars.

Dad reminded her that a cougar had to eat winter and summer the same as us.

One night while we were at the supper table we heard a cougar make a kill. There was the scream of a cougar and the bleat of a deer and then silence.

"I suppose you are going to tell me that was a screech owl," snipped Mother, still ruffled from her first night in camp when what she still felt was a cougar on the roof Dad declared was a screech owl. Dad admitted that what we had heard was no screech owl.

"That's Old Jack," he said, "and it's about time someone hunted him down." Old Jack was sort of an alarming fixture around camp. He'd follow people at night walking the county road or taking the railroad track down to Potter and Chester's. Mr. George Brunner, superintendent of Potter and Chester's, always carried a stout piece of limb when he and his wife, Peggy (she used to be Marguerite Pinnell, my second grade teacher), would walk the three miles up the railroad track to our camp to see Mother and Dad.

"A cougar is a cat and just as curious," Mr. Brunner used to tell Mother and Mrs. Brunner but they weren't convinced and neither was I. Mother and I never went out to our outhouse after dark. Instead we would use the pot under the bed. Sometimes it was all I could do to hold it when we had company. I had to hold it because I couldn't go in the pot with company right there and I would rather wet my pants than go out in the dark to the outhouse.

One time Old Jack crossed the railroad track right in front of Mr. and Mrs. Brunner. Mrs. Brunner said she was so startled she forgot to scream. Mr. Brunner said if she had she would have scared the life out of Old Jack because she could scream louder than any cougar.

One thing about that incident, it ended Mother and Dad's walks down to Potter and Chester's to visit the Brunners.

"I'll ride the log train," declared Mother.

Old Jack ended up being a real nuisance along with a cousin of his, a bobcat that began hanging around and had the same bad habit of following people. Mr. Brunner finally advised parents to keep their younger children in the house until he could come up with a solution. Cougar hunting is no simple thing. You may see one often but the cougar always seems to plan those meetings for a time when you don't have a gun.

The acknowledged cougar hunter in our area was Mr. Baumgartner, the Olney rancher. Mr. Baumgartner had trained cougar hounds and could go through the forest afoot like a breath of wind. Mr. Brunner got hold of Mr. Baumgartner. Mr. Baumgartner put his dogs on the trail of Old Jack and they didn't catch up with him until they reached Jewell, ten miles over the mountains from our camp, in the Nehalem Valley. That ended the career of Old Jack. Mr. Baumgartner said he and his dogs had done the old veteran a favor because he was so old he had lost the use of several teeth and eventually might have attacked humans, especially children, in order to survive.

"And to think he was right on our roof," gasped Mother. That almost got an argument started with Dad but he acted as though he hadn't heard and Mother let it pass. With Old Jack gone, the nights were more quiet for a time around the camp, but a new cougar moved in, taking over the territory left free by the death of Old Jack. There were still plenty of bobcats, bear, coyote, deer, mink, otter, beaver, rats, weasels, mice, and wandering cattle around to make the outside areas interesting. I'll get around to the cattle later.

Although venison and bear meat were the main supplementary foods provided by nature, there were ample wild foods if one knew how to prepare them. These included watercress, dandelions, bracken fern, fireweed, sour grass, elderberries, blackberries, huckleberries, and even alder bark and Douglas fir.

Mother was used to getting her spring vegetables at a market but relying on nature was handier and her seasons were earlier. You had to know, however, what to harvest and when and how. The camp women finally found something that Mother didn't know one bit about.

"Ain't you ever et dandelions?" asked Mrs. Johnson.

"Only as Daddy O'Hoyt's wine," said Mother.

There were lots of wild mushrooms around but Mother wouldn't touch anything like that for fear of getting poisonous toadstools, of which there were also plenty.

None of nature's gift items really attracted Mother but she was a staunch believer in spring greens as body toners and tonics and after a long winter practically void of greens of any kind she was anxious to learn how to harvest and prepare the early spring greens available.

Dad had no use for any of them. He didn't even like lettuce but Mother insisted the body needed roughage and one of the most pleasant ways to get it was in salads. Dad was strictly meat, potato, and gravy with pie, cake, and puddings for toppers.

Until he met and married Mother there was no room in his diet for greens, although he did like things such as carrots, parsnips, and cabbage.

I was familiar with sour grass and watercress because we kids used to eat them when out playing along the creek or exploring in the woods. Watercress grew in backwater pools where the water moved slowly but was clear. Sour grass was found along stream banks as well as back in the heavily wooded areas. Both were good as salads or mixed with other greens.

Dandelions had to be picked when the leaves were young and tender. Mrs. Lillich taught Mother how to spot the good ones and how to wash and trim them and cook them for twenty minutes or so with lots of water and with maybe bacon added for flavor. Mother served them with butter and vinegar just like spinach. Dad would almost gag at the sight of them and so would I but they really tasted pretty good. It was difficult to admit that to Mother but she could tell from our clean plates that they weren't as bad as we let on.

The very young shoots of fireweed picked before the flowers appeared tasted something like asparagus when peeled but Mother didn't serve them often. They could be eaten raw, which Mother said was good because cooking often ruined the health-giving stuff in greens and vegetables.

Miner's lettuce was more difficult to find but it was a good substitute for real lettuce, which didn't appear on the market until summer.

Some of the women cooked the very young leaves of nettles but I never trusted nettles and neither did Mother. We had gotten stung too many times by nettle leaves. Anyway, Dad set his foot down hard enough to shake the whole house when Mother suggested nettles. Any logger who worked on the rigging and spent his days surrounded by devil's-club and nettles among other things wasn't about to go home and have nettles for supper.

"Jesus Christ, no!" he blurted out when Mother showed him a batch of nettle leaves Mrs. Boyle had brought over.

"That's no way to talk in front of Samuel," Mother repri-
manded him. "That's no way to talk, anyway," she added.

"I eat enough grass and weeds as it is," Dad snorted, "but
when you go adding nettles that's enough." Mother agreed, so I
still don't know whether nettle leaves in your stomach would
smart like when they touch your hand or not. The Boyle girls
said they didn't but girls don't know a lot of things, so I never
tried them, even at Lena Boyle's house. Even when she had a
kettle of them cooking on the stove one day and offered me
some.

It seemed strange to eat parts of trees but Mrs. Johnson could
make a passable tea by steeping Douglas fir needles in boiling
water. She also used the inner bark of alder trees for something
that tasted awful. The tea intrigued Mother and she made some
for Dad because she read someplace that it contained Vitamin
C. Mother said Vitamin C was what you got from oranges and
lemons but that Douglas fir tea would be a lot cheaper. Dad said
he didn't care how cheap it was. He told Mother that when she
made tea he wanted Lipton's, and no Douglas fir needles or
alder bark mixed in.

When summer came and farm produce from Olney and the
Astoria area arrived on the market, relationships improved rapidly between husbands and wives in the camp along with the
menus.

During the summer months we always had a vegetable gar-
den. Dad cleared a space in the underbrush behind the house.
We used to plant carrots, beets, tomatoes, spuds, lettuce, cab-
bage, and sometimes ear corn. During World War I, Miss Della
Brown, my first grade teacher, encouraged us kids to plant vic-
tory gardens. Our dads cleared a spot near the creek down by
Mrs. Johnson's house. I think the rats, birds, mice, rabbits, and
Fen and Jake got more of the vegetables than we did.

Mr. Casey caught Fen and Jake eating Mae Casey's fresh ripe
tomatoes off the vine. He yanked them, squirming and fighting,

before their mother. It so happened she had one of Mae's tomatoes in her mouth.

Mr. Casey was a real deputy sheriff, deputized by the authorities in Astoria so he could protect us against I.W.W.s or any other lawbreakers that needed special handling at the Western Cooperage. Mr. Casey was a big man and he could be rough. He knew Mrs. Johnson had to be eating one of Mae's tomatoes because Mae was the only one that had any ripe ones. He took his deputy sheriff's badge from his overalls pocket and pinned it on the bib. Then he broke off a good length of willow switch. I was right there and it made me want to wet my pants just watching him, he was so calm and deliberate.

"Casey, you ain't layin' a switch to my boys," Mrs. Johnson challenged. Mr. Casey said he didn't intend to.

"Then what the hell's that switch for?" asked Mrs. Johnson.

"For you," said Mr. Casey, walking toward Mrs. Johnson and Fen and Jake. "I'm going to turn you over my knee and put a row of welts on your hind end that you'll remember every time you eat a raw tomato." Mrs. Johnson's mouth dropped open and her corncob pipe fell to the ground. She could see Mr. Casey was mighty serious.

"Casey, you sonofabitch," shouted Mrs. Johnson, "you take one more step and I'll have the law on you." Mr. Casey took a half-dozen more steps.

"I am the law," he reminded her. Mrs. Johnson ran for the house, jumped inside, and slammed the door shut. It didn't have a lock but I could hear her shoving chairs and stuff against it.

"You touch this door and I'll blow your goddamn head off," she screamed at Mr. Casey. Mr. Casey said if she did that she would really be in trouble, shooting at a man of the law. I don't think I had ever been so excited in my life. This was more exciting than the fight to the death between Prince and Tag. I didn't really think Mrs. Johnson would shoot Mr. Casey and I didn't think Mr. Casey would bend Mrs. Johnson over his knee, but then you never can tell about grownups.

Finally I could hear Mrs. Johnson pushing aside the things she had shoved in front of the door. The door opened and she stood in the doorway, calm as a rock and no longer frightened, with feet apart and arms akimbo.

"I ain't never run from trouble," she announced loftily. "Now just what the hell *do* you want?" she said, staring at Mr. Casey like a cougar cat about to jump a deer. Mr. Casey wasn't awed one little bit.

"I want welts on the asses of Fen and Jake and I want you to put 'em there and I want 'em there now," said Mr. Casey.

Mrs. Johnson eyed Mr. Casey a moment, looked over at Fen and Jake, and then stepped outside to retrieve her corncob pipe. With the pipe back in her mouth she reached for the switch Mr. Casey was still holding. She said she had a better idea.

"You boys told me them tomatoes was from our garden," she said, flicking the tip of the willow switch in a menacing motion. "Now, that's lyin' and if they's one thing the old man and me won't put up with, it's lyin'." I never saw Mrs. Johnson look so stern. "Now, I want a couple of bare behinds looking me right in the face," she ordered, "and, Fen, I want you to lay this switch on Jake three times, and, Jake, I want you to do the same by Fen. And don't try to do it easy because me and Casey is watchin'." With that she handed the willow switch to Fen and ordered him to lay it on. Fen began to bawl and so did Jake. "I ain't goin' to wait long," cautioned Mrs. Johnson.

Mr. Casey was having second thoughts. "Maybe one good welt would teach 'em a lesson," he suggested with a guilty pitch to his voice.

Mrs. Johnson turned on him like a she cat protecting her kittens.

"You're worse than a goddamn old woman," she snarled. "You raise your kids and I'll raise mine." Turning back to Fen, she told him once more to "lay it on." He did. I could see the welts pop up on Jake's bare behind. When it was Jake's turn to lay the whip to Fen he did it with relish. After the third lash the two

143

boys went at it tooth and toenail with pants down around their ankles.

"You bastard," shrilled Fen, "you laid that switch on as hard as you could."

"Ma was a watchin'," bawled Jake.

"You satisfied?" Mrs. Johnson asked Mr. Casey. Mr. Casey nodded with a smile.

"I'm damn glad you weren't my ma," he added with a grin.

When I told Dad and Mother what happened Dad said a lot of camp people would have paid good money to watch. He said it would have been more upright than Mother's charging the camp people for ice cream. I think Dad was still put out because Mother forgot to hold back some ice cream for us.

Be that as it may, Mother set one of the nicest tables in the camp. Some folks felt she was putting on airs when she insisted we eat off a tablecloth. Our table was set with good Boston dishes instead of the heavy crockery or enamel dishware that most families used. The knives, forks, and spoons were always in their proper spots and she early taught me how to set the table and that became one of my jobs, the same as filling the wood-box, stacking wood, and helping Dad chop kindling.

Although logging camp homes were usually unpainted and rough on the outside most of them were warm, friendly, and comfortable on the inside. Mother and Dad took special care with ours. The floor covering was linoleum but once a year the furniture was shoved into a tight fit at one end while Mother and Dad applied Valspar finish to the other end. After an application it fairly glistened. After the first application was dry the furniture was moved to the treated end and the operation repeated.

The linoleum in most logging camp homes was pock-marked by the pointed calks loggers wore in the soles of their shoes ("cork" shoes in logger terminology instead of "calk" shoes). Dad never wore his calk shoes in the house. He either took them

144

off and left them on the porch or strapped pieces of board to the bottoms of his shoes so the calks wouldn't touch the linoleum.

There was a throw rug by my cot and another on the floor beside Dad and Mother's bed so when you hopped out of bed on a winter morning your bare feet wouldn't hit the ice-cold linoleum.

I loved our home. The inside of most camp homes was unfinished, with the studding peering out at you, bare, stark, and skeleton-like. Mother and Dad papered the inside of our house with plain gray, heavy felt building paper. It added to the warmth of the room as well as improving its looks. Mother broke the monotony of the plain gray color with framed pictures, little hanging wall shelves, and a big framed oval photograph of me taken when I was about five years old. It hung right above my cot and folks who came to visit were always saying how much it looked like me. Of course, that was silly because it was me. That was what I told Mrs. Jacobson once and Mother made me apologize and then go outside. She told me later it was bad manners to belittle people and that was what I had done to Mrs. Jacobson.

Plenty of wood in the woodbox, plenty of food on hand, and a wife who enjoyed cooking was what it took to keep up with the appetite of a logger. Men such as Dad who were on the run most of the day, uphill and downhill, through brush and on and off logs, took a lot of fueling. Mother said a man like Dad required about 9,000 calories a day. An ordinary laborer in the camp or in Astoria would need around 6,500. An office worker of that period would take in 3,000 to 4,000.

When Mother first came to the camp as a bride the remoteness and the necessity to lay in ample supplies of food for the winter months made her uneasy. She sought out Mrs. Johnson and asked her advice.

"They's one thing to remember," cautioned Mrs. Johnson. "This is fart and tater country." That was a new expression to Mother. She hadn't yet had time to adjust to Mrs. Johnson and some of her quaint, and totally original, thoughts, philosophies, and expressions.

"That means bean and spud country," explained Mrs. Johnson in answer to Mother's request for a clarification. Her advice was that with plenty of dry beans and potatoes on hand a body wasn't likely to go hungry and most certainly wouldn't starve no matter what happened with the weather. The camp women canned dozens of quarts of wild berries and domestic fruits and vegetables in the summer. They always had an extra hundred-pound sack of sugar and forty-nine-pound sack of flour set aside for emergencies. Dried onions and prunes were handy, as were plenty of rice, beans, spuds, coffee, tea, oatmeal, syrup, Karo, vinegar, baking powder, baking soda, salt, pepper, and spices. Dad could get along without a lot of things but pepper wasn't one of them. He put pepper on everything from corn on the cob to rice and Mother swore he would put it on apple pie if she would let him.

With the help of Mrs. Johnson, Mrs. Lillich, and the other camp women Mother got through that first winter with no major shortages. Dad did run out of chewing tobacco in January and that irritated him because then he had to buy it at the company commissary and Mr. Bramble charged more than Ross, Higgins and Company in Astoria. Each time he would go to the commissary for tobacco he would come home in such a bad mood that Mother never again let him run out.

Mother had spent a lifetime cooking with gas and suddenly there wasn't a cookstove within twenty miles that didn't burn wood.

"You can use all you want and it costs practically nothing," Dad cheerfully informed her.

For weeks and weeks whatever Dad ate was either cooked black or half raw.

"The only good meal your husband is getting is his chew of tobacco," Mrs. Kneeland told her. With the aid of the other women in camp Mother eventually learned the knack of cooking

146

with wood. Pitchy wood built up a hot fire fast for quick heating of water and for frying; dry alder was good for baking, although you had to keep an eye on the firebox because alder burned fast; regular fir or hemlock was fine for sustained cooking such as roasts, baking potatoes, and such. All of that was not too difficult to master. The hard part was learning how much of which kind of wood to put in the stove for any particular chore. By the time I was old enough to know what I was eating Mother was rated as one of the better cooks in camp.

Among her favorite dishes, and Dad's too, was Boston baked beans baked in a genuine bean pot from Boston. Dad could just about eat a whole crock of Mother's Boston baked beans. I preferred the Western kind that came in a tin can. That was almost like being a traitor. Mother's pies and puddings were heavenly and her cookies were big, thick, and almost a meal at snack time. She also got to be an expert with doughnuts. Ida O'Hoyt was always marveling at Mother's doughnuts.

"You ain't much with bear and you can't tell bear from venison but by golly there's no one can beat you at making doughnuts," Mrs. O'Hoyt used to say, smacking her lips over a hot, crisp-shelled doughnut right out of the frying oil. When Mother made doughnuts the odor seemed to drift across the entire camp and we always had more callers then than any time.

Dad was proud of Mother's cooking ability. He said if a Boston lady could beat these old logging camp hands at their own stoves, then by George she was a real Westerner. Mother used to reply that the day she married Dad was when she became a Westerner. Dad liked to hear that. Then he'd sometimes go over and lift Mother right off her feet and give her a big smack. She'd squeal and make all kinds of funny sounds.

It was about then that they always sent me outside.

It seemed to me they were always sending me outside. I asked Mrs. Johnson if she and Mr. Johnson ever sent Fen and Jake outside. She said, sometimes but that I shouldn't worry about being sent outside.

"One of these days you'll understand why," she predicted, "and by that time I bet you have a baby brother."

I told Mother what Mrs. Johnson said and asked if I was going to really have a baby brother?

Mother's face turned the color of ripe elderberries and she said I should pay no mind to Mrs. Johnson and her gossip.

After that I didn't get sent outside any more.

And I never got a baby brother, either.

Or even a sister.

16
Bull in the Schoolyard

Almost as scary in the middle of the night as the call of a cougar was the sound of a cowbell. Maybe it was because it was so out of place in the middle of a thousand square miles of forest. Or maybe it was because experience had taught us that with the sound of the bell there was always a bull—big, mean, and usually a Holstein.

The sound of a bell and the thump of cattle hoofs on railroad ties and track ballast always drew an expletive or two from Dad. He could snore through the caterwauling of a cougar on our roof but the sound of a cowbell would jerk him upright out of a sound sleep. Mother said it was because he spent so many years on Grandpa Churchill's farm. After years in logging camps he was still alert to escaping cows.

The cattle that came to our camp would invade us two or three times a year and usually came in spring or summer and from the Olney area. Sometimes they belonged to Mr. Baumgartner and sometimes to other farmers in the area. But wherever they came from they were always accompanied by a bull and it was always a mean one. Dad said the green grass along the railroad right of way probably attracted them and they would strain so hard to reach it they would sometimes break down their pasture fence. Once free they would follow the grass feed the ten miles from Olney right into our camp. Train crews would often see them and alert us that they were coming. Their owners would just sit back and let them follow the railroad until they reached the camp. Then they could drive them home by the county road.

Whenever a herd arrived at camp it seemed to head for the camp vegetable gardens. I guess they were like Mother. They were hungry for greens and a change of diet.

I remember awakening one night to the sound of a cowbell. Every herd had one cow with a bell around her neck. The farmer could tell where his loose cattle were by following the sound of the bell.

On this particular night the herd was lumbering around in our garden. Every now and then the bull or one of the other animals would stumble against the house and make the dishes rattle. I could hear Dad's feet hit the floor as he swung himself out of bed. He came thumping in his nightgown and slippers past my cot and over to the kitchen stove, where he had a lantern hanging on the wall. He lifted the lantern from its nail on the wall, lit it, and grabbed a big chunk of stovewood. Mother was right behind him, worried and frightened.

"Don't go out there, Sam," she kept pleading, "there's a bull there."

"They'll trample our garden to pieces," said Dad. "I got me a hefty stick. All I got to do is get the bell cow moving and the rest will follow." Mother kept pleading but it wasn't any use. Dad was mad and his mind was made up. Out the door he went in his nightgown and slippers and clutching the lantern and the stovewood club.

Mother and I went from window to window following his progress by the trail of the lighted lantern. We really didn't need the lantern because Dad was shouting, cussing, and thumping rear ends and heads with the chunk of stovewood. We could hear cattle crashing through the underbrush in an effort to avoid Dad's club.

Pretty soon there was an angry snort and then a bellow. Mother gripped my arm until it hurt.

"It's the bull," she breathed almost in a whisper. About that time we could hear Dad's club hitting home. Then the night air was filled with bull bellows and Dad's bellows. We heard the crash of glass and Dad's lantern went out but his voice and the thump of wood against flesh continued. The bull was still bellowing but Dad had him out of the garden and on the railroad track by now. Mother and I could follow the action by Dad's white nightshirt. Dad never let the bull get set. He kept hammering him with the piece of stovewood and the bull was either stumbling over the ties and uneven ballast of the track or getting mired down in the drain ditches that ran along both sides of the right of way.

By this time the wild commotion had roused everyone in the area including Mr. Robinson and Mr. Irving. They both arrived on the scene with lighted lanterns just in time to help Dad rout the bull. The cows were scattered throughout the underbrush surrounding the camp, and over in the direction of the schoolhouse the bell cow's bell was clanging.

Mr. Robinson and Mr. Irving came home with Dad so he could have some lantern light. Dad asked them to come in. Mother scooted back into bed and under the covers and I hurried under the covers of my cot. The three men came into the house and Dad lighted a lamp. Mr. Robinson looked around and then sat in Dad's big rocking chair.

"Damn me if this ain't familiar," he said, rocking and looking at Dad. "You in your nightshirt, Caroline hiding under the covers, me and Jim routed out of bed. The only thing changed is this time you've got Samuel and it was a bull instead of a screech owl that caused all the ruckus." Dad got a silly grin on his face and admitted it was something of a coincidence.

Mr. Robinson replied that ordinarily it would be a coincidence but in the case of Dad and Mother he didn't know.

"I'm beginning to think you just like to jump out of bed in the middle of the night in your nightshirt and start bellerin'," said Mr. Robinson, still rocking.

"You seen the bull," protested Dad. "This wasn't no screech owl scarin' Caroline, this was fifteen hundred pounds of cantankerous, mean, dirt-pawing Holstein bull," said Dad. "You seen him."

"I seen him," agreed Mr. Robinson, "and he is big, and he is mean, and he is a Holstein. But goddammit, Sam, what we usually do in these cases is get several men with lanterns and just sort of ease the cattle down to the county road and get them headed home. That way they'd be home in a couple of days, bull and all."

He stopped rocking and got to his feet. "Now," he continued, "they's scattered from hell to breakfast in the underbrush and God only knows where that sonofabitchin' bull is." With that he and Mr. Irving marched out of the house. Dad crawled back under the covers beside Mother.

"I don't care what you and T.W. say," declared Mother, "that creature on the roof my first night in camp was a cougar, not a screech owl."

"Dammit, Carrie, go to sleep," grumbled Dad.

The next morning early, we learned where the cows and the bull were. They were in the schoolyard and had Fen and Jake Johnson treed up a stump.

Miss Marjorie Stearns, the teacher, came running up the track to our house. Her hair was flying and she was all out of breath. Mother sat her down on my cot and got her a dipper of water from the bucket. She calmed down a bit and began to talk.

She said Fen and Jake had the job of starting the fire in the stove every morning to warm up the school. She decided to go to the school a little early and when she got close enough to see it she noticed there was no wood smoke coming out of the stove-pipe. She was saying some nasty things to herself about Fen and Jake when she heard the tinkle of a cowbell. She began going a little slower and then she saw Fen and Jake sitting atop a big stump that was in the schoolyard. They both saw her and waved her back.

"Don't come up here," yelled Fen, "they's a goddamn bull and a bunch of cows here. The bull ran us up this stump. He's mean."

Mother told Miss Stearns they had better go up and see Mr. Bramble. Mr. Bramble was not at all sympathetic. When he heard the bull had Fen and Jake marooned on top of a stump all he did was laugh.

"You've got to do something," snapped Mother, "the children can't go to school."

"I don't have to do anything," said Mr. Bramble, "I get paid to run this office and keep books, not chase bulls out of school-yards."

Just then Mr. Robinson came in, so Mother and Miss Stearns told him what had happened. It seemed to tickle him, too, that the bull had Fen and Jake up a stump. He said he would round up a few men and chase the cattle down to the county road and get them headed back toward Olney and home.

"Where's Sam?" he asked.

"He's at work," said Mother, looking a little perplexed.

"Good," said Mr. Robinson. Mother looked even more per-plexed.

"T.W. can say the funniest things," she said, looking at Miss Stearns and shaking her head.

Mr. Robinson gathered up a half-dozen men from the ma-chine shop. They picked up a few stout limbs for clubs and a couple of empty galvanized buckets to beat on with sticks. When they got to the school they began yelling and beating on the buckets. The cows tore out through the underbrush toward the county road. The bull acted as though he might argue but after a few snorts and a little dirt-pawing to save face, he turned tail and followed the cows. The men followed them through the brush and out to the road, keeping up a terrible din that you could hear clear up to the machine shop. When it looked as though the cows wouldn't turn back the men gave up the chase and came back to work.

There were cow patties all over the schoolyard after the cows left. After a couple of days in the sun they dried out and the boys had great fun breaking off pieces to throw at the girls. Miss Stearns finally made them stop. Jake Johnson even ate a tiny bit of one patty. I asked him what it tasted like.

"Shit," he answered.

I wasn't yet going to school when the cow and bull incident occurred but my friend Rex Gaynor and I had already attended classes for a few days. We were still a year too young to start but we used to sit on the school porch and listen to what went on inside. During school periods it got kind of lonely around camp because all the bigger kids were in school and all that was left was babies and little kids who couldn't even climb a tree. So, after part of a morning's play, Rex and I began hanging around the school, peeking into the room through a space between the doorjamb and the door, and sitting on the porch waiting for school to let out.

One day Miss Stearns came out and asked if we would like to come inside and sit at a desk. We watched Fen and Jake try to do an arithmetic problem on the blackboard in front of the class; watched Bert Hathaway rise up from his desk at eleven o'clock and announce to Miss Stearns and the rest of the class, "My breadbasket is empty. I'm going home and eat." And he did. In fact Bert went home every day at eleven o'clock instead of noon like everyone else. Mae Casey was there and so were Phil Peets, one of the Boyle girls, and two or three others.

Rex and I had such a good time in school we begged our mothers to let us go some more. They said to ask Miss Stearns.

There were three or four unoccupied desks, so she said we could if we would stay in our seats and be quiet.

We did that for most of the school week but then it began to get boring. When Mother called me to go to school I told her I wasn't going. She said I was. That was a nasty turn of affairs. I told her I had had enough of school.

I guess Mother and Mrs. Gaynor had talked things over because Rex had to keep going to school, too. When recess came we went exploring along Klaskanine Creek between our camp and the Fischer and Leitzel camp. It was crawdad season and there were a lot of crawfish in the creek. We didn't catch them to eat because most of them were too small. We just caught them for fun. Well, we were having so much fun overturning rocks in the creek and catching crawdads we forgot all about recess and school. And we probably wouldn't have remembered then except that we heard both our mothers calling us.

"Now we're going to get it," predicted Rex.

"Maybe we should take some crawdads home to cook and eat," I suggested. Rex shook his head.

"Why don't we tell our mothers we got lost?" he said.

"That would be lying," I reminded him.

We decided the best thing to do was get home as quick as possible and tell the truth. We were having so much fun we forgot about school.

Our mothers were relieved when they saw us run out of the woods and up the railroad track toward home and they didn't seem mad when we told them we were hunting crawdads and forgot about school. I thought maybe we wouldn't have to go back but Mother spoiled that hope.

"One lesson you have to learn is finish what you start," she admonished. She said we begged and begged to go to school but now after three days we wanted to quit. She said we would have to finish out the week. Mrs. Gaynor agreed.

I tried to argue that if a body was supposed to finish what he started why couldn't we go back to the creek and finish catching crawdads?

Mother countered that you finished first things first.

Finishing what you start was one of life's precepts, according to Mother. On our woods walks she was always pointing out things like birds building nests; Paddy the Beaver building a dam or gnawing down a tree; Striped Chipmunk gathering a winter's supply of food; bees gathering nectar for honey. In nature, she said, if you didn't finish what you started you might go hungry all winter, or have to sit out in the cold, or even die.

We kids had put a pulley on a long piece of discarded straw line (small steel cable used in logging) and anchored the line to stumps on each side of a small gulley. We then hooked a rope to the pulley and would swing across the gulley, dangling from the rope while the pulley followed the straw line from one side of the gulley to the other side.

Mother used our skyline as a demonstration of finishing what you start. If we had anchored one end of the straw line and then wandered off on some other project before anchoring the other end we wouldn't have our skyline, she pointed out.

It was mighty hard to argue with Mother, she was always so logical. Besides, she was clerk of the Western Cooperage school district so knew a lot about school and education. Mrs. Robinson told me I had a mighty smart mother and should do as she told me. All my schoolteachers thought Mother was real smart and they used to like to come to our house and eat and talk and sometimes listen to the Victrola.

It's a funny thing, being smart. Mother, now, had been to high school, could read and write, loved good music, and knew about etiquette and good manners, but she couldn't tell bear meat from venison. Mrs. Johnson, on the other hand, cussed a lot, could barely read or write, and ate spaghetti with her fingers, but she could tell bear meat from venison.

I asked Mother about that. She said that was because there were a lot of ways to be smart. She said Dad couldn't read very well but he was smart. He could move a steam donkey engine from one setting to another, up steep slopes and across canyons. She said Dad could do that but Mr. Jack Smith, the big boss in Portland, couldn't do it, at least not without working in the woods for a time and learning. The same thing applied to his job and Dad.

That was one of the things I liked about Mother. She always had an answer for any question I asked. Even as to where babies come from. When I asked her that she told me.

"You'll have all these kids out in the bushes screwin'," shouted Mrs. Johnson after Fen and Jake told her what I had told them.

"Some of them already are, your Fen included," Mother shot back.

"Fen?" Mrs. Johnson stopped with her mouth half open. She stared, puzzled, and then smiled. "Well, I'll be damned. He's going to be as bad as his old man."

17
The Day the Sun Went Out

Folks at the Western Cooperage camp had an excellent working relationship with nature. Wind, rain, thunder, lightning, floods, earth slides, blistering hot summer sun, mud, dust, and trees they understood.

They could cope with most any barrier nature might set up to protect her forests, including a topsy-turvy terrain crossed and crisscrossed by canyons that could hide a city and peaks and ridges that seemed to hold up the sky.

When Dad left the Maine woods in 1902 to come West the old logger boss for whom he had worked a half-dozen seasons as a chopper tried to discourage him.

"I been out there," he told Dad, "and it's the goddamndest country I ever seen. If you ain't climbin' up you're climbin' down. And if you want to set they's hardly a level place big enough to put your ass."

Despite the obstacles nature put in his way the logger pushed deeper and deeper into the heart of the Coast Range. His powerful machines, mounted on massive log sleds so they could pull themselves up, down, or across almost any kind of terrain, were crashing their way across virgin foothills of the mighty Cascades.

"They's damn few places a Humboldt yarder with a good

man at the throttle and steam in its boiler can't go," Uncle Marsh used to brag to Aunt Blanche. And what he said was true. I have seen a big Humboldt on its two hundred tons of sled on a ridge top so narrow they had to anchor it to stumps with steel cables to keep it from sliding back down the slope it had just pulled itself up.

Year by year the machines seemed to get bigger, faster, and more complex. The ultimate was the multi-unit skidder mounted on railroad trucks. A skidder, with its three separate engines fed by one huge boiler, its hundred-foot steel tower, and its dozen or so drums for reeling in cables, could weigh up to three hundred tons and could devastate forty acres in a matter of days. It usually took a couple of hefty Shay locomotives to move a skidder, its tons of blocks, lines, and other rigging, and the two dozen or so skilled men who made up its crew.

If a logger came to some obstacle he couldn't go over he went around or tunneled through. If a canyon got in his way he filled it in or built a trestle. If there was a log on the other side, come hell or high water he was going to get it.

"One of these days we are going to be out of trees," predicted Mother.

"You and me will never see that day," was Dad's impatient and rather tart answer.

"Maybe not," insisted Mother, "but Samuel will." That quieted Dad and set him to thinking.

We were on a high ridge northeast of the Western Cooperage headquarters camp, waiting for a total eclipse of the sun. It was the afternoon of June 8, 1918, and we had ridden up to this new logging area on high ground for a better view. Mrs. Johnson along with Fen and Jake and several other wives and mothers had come. Mr. Foss Cox said he hadn't had so many women in the cab of his locomotive since last wild blackberry season, which usually came in July.

Although the camp people got along fine with nature for the most part, the immensity and remoteness of space was beyond the reach of most to imagine or cope with. Mrs. Johnson included.

Her curiosity aroused by Mother, she wanted to know all there was to know about space and the coming eclipse. Mother was almost as much in the dark as everyone else about what lay beyond the blanket of stars that seemed to crowd in almost at treetop level on a clear, summer night. But she did know something about eclipses and what she knew she tried to pass on to Mrs. Johnson. She told Mrs. Johnson we could expect a full, or almost full, eclipse and when that moment came the camp would be dark even though it would only be four o'clock in the afternoon.

"You mean the sun is going to go out?" Mrs. Johnson asked, a note of uneasiness creeping into her voice.

Mother assured her it wasn't but because it would get dark it would seem so.

"I ain't never seen nothin' like this before," Mrs. Johnson admitted. "I'll be glad when God gets things straightened out." Mother said she could rest assured that God knew what He was doing and nothing bad would happen.

It was while we were waiting for the eclipse that Mother and Dad got to talking about logging and what was happening to Oregon's and Clatsop County's forests. Mother pointed to numerous plumes of smoke and steam that marked steam donkey locations. Dad said the smokes over by Wickiup Mountain were from Big Creek Logging Company; the ones in the broad basin in front of us up toward Fog Mountain were the California Barrel; from our height we could see over toward Saddle Mountain and the logging shows of Crown Willamette Paper Company, Eastern Western, and others Dad couldn't identify.

"They's a lot of donkeys scattered around," he finally admitted. He was silent for a time, saying nothing, just looking. "You best be something other than a logger, Samuel," he said, finally, smiling and patting my head. "Maybe an engineer, like your mother wants, who builds roads and bridges and things."

I said I liked logging the best but maybe I could be a police-man like they had in Astoria and Portland, or a hunter like Mr. Slater. Dad said a policeman would be good.

Mother opened the face cover of the gold watch she carried on a chain around her neck. It had a tiny picture of Dad and me inside the face cover and it had Roman numerals instead of regular numbers. Mother said as soon as I learned to tell time better she and Dad would buy me a real Ingersoll pocket watch such as Dad and most loggers carried. They cost around a dollar.

"It's getting near time," she announced, closing the face cover and picking up some pieces of smoked glass she had brought along.

"Don't look at the sun with your bare eyes," she warned, "use a smoked glass." She gave me one and Dad one and one each for Mrs. Johnson and Fen and Jake. She had a few extras but the other women all had their own.

We looked at the sun through the smoked glass and sure enough there was a big shadow that covered a fourth of it. Some of the loggers came over and looked through our pieces of glass. Pretty soon you could tell it was getting darker.

In a little while it was dark as anything and you could see stars.

"Caroline," Mrs. Johnson called out, "I'm getting kind of scared." Mother told her it would start getting light pretty quick and not to worry. Dad and I weren't a bit scared and neither were Fen and Jake. When it was all over and daylight again Mrs. Johnson came over to Mother.

"This is a day when I oughta put something in the Family Book," she said. She shook her head in fascination as she recalled what she had just witnessed. "Never in my borned days did I expect to see the sun go out."

I could see Mother start to remind her that the sun didn't really go out, but she dropped the question. Instead she asked about the "Family Book."

"Do you have a family Bible?" Mother asked.

Mrs. Johnson nodded. "We keep it in the trunk. It's just too damned big for a body to read."

It was getting about time for the crew to quit and get aboard the crew cars for the train ride back to camp. We got on the cars with the men. I happened to sit beside Mr. Irving, the woods boss. Mr. Irving had a big, old Airedale dog that he kept tied up while he was at work. Rex and I used to visit him a lot. His name was Roger and he seemed to like us as much as we liked him.

I asked Mr. Irving if it would be all right if Rex and me sometimes took Roger for a walk. Mr. Irving said Roger would like that but for us to be sure we had a tight grip on his rope tether because Roger was a strong dog.

A couple of days after the eclipse Rex and I went up to see Roger. I told Rex what Mr. Irving had said.

"Let's take him for a walk now," Rex suggested. It seemed like a good idea, so we untied the rope tether from the alder tree Mr. Irving always anchored it to and started out. Roger was eager to run and wet and run some more but we kept a firm hold on the rope. We led him up to Rex's house to show Mrs. Gaynor and then down the railroad track to our house to show my mother. We were just about to our house when one of Lena Boyle's half-grown cats strolled through an open door, out onto the porch, and then down to the two long planks that served as a bridge across the railroad drain ditch. When Roger saw that cat he started right out like Mr. Casey's Shay locomotive and there wasn't anything that Rex and I could do but go along. We kept yelling and trying to stop him but it was no use. He had the pulling power of one of Mr. Baumgartner's work horses.

When the cat saw Roger headed its way it scampered back across the planks, up the steps, across the porch, and back into the house. Roger, towing Rex and me, was right on its tail. We went lunging through Lena Boyle's living-dining room and right into the kitchen where Lena and a couple of other women were sitting at the kitchen table having coffee.

When Roger towing Rex and me came bursting in we really startled those women. Roger got the cat cornered behind the cookstove and bored right in after it. He rammed his head and shoulders into the space between the stove and the wall and forced the stove aside so he could get in. Well, he reached right in there, picked that squalling cat up in his mouth, backed out, and when he was in the clear shook his head like a fox terrier with a rat. Rex and I were bawling and Lena and the other two women were screaming. It was a terrible mess, especially when Mother heard the ruckus and came running over.

By that time the little cat was lying on the floor with a broken back. When Mother saw the cat she was no help because she started bawling and carrying on something fierce. Lena Boyle kept screaming, "Do something, do something." It was all Rex and I could do to hold Roger. Now that he had taken care of Lena's cat he was anxious to get back outside and run some more and wet. He pulled Rex and me right back outside and down the track we went. I could hear Mother, and Lena, and the other two women carrying on clear down to the crossing.

There was no holding Roger now. He was really fired up. As we approached Aunt Blanche and Uncle Marshall's house Rex and I were taking two railroad ties at each step, Roger was going so fast. Aunt Blanche had heard all the yelling, so she was outside. When we got near enough she grabbed on to Roger's rope and with her hanging on we got him stopped.

Aunt Blanche helped us get Roger back up to Mr. Irving's place and safely tied to his alder tree. When we got back down to Lena Boyle's she and Mother and the other women were standing outside on the railroad track. Mother said the poor little cat was still alive and lying on the kitchen floor. None of the women would go near it. Mother sent me and Rex to get Mrs. Johnson. Mrs. Johnson yelled for Jake, so he came along with his .22 rifle and shot it. The bullet left a hole in Lena's linoleum but she said she didn't mind. She was still sobbing.

Jake picked up the dead cat and Lena asked if we boys would bury it. Jake wanted to know why we couldn't just toss it out in the brush. All of the women, even Mrs. Johnson, gave him such a terrible look, he said he would bury it.

You would have thought that with the cat buried that would end the matter. But it didn't.

When Mr. Boyle and the other men came home from work Lena had to tell Mr. Boyle about everything that had happened and Mother was doing the same with Dad. But she wasn't mad, whereas Lena Boyle was. I guess between the time Jake and us buried the cat and the time Mr. Boyle got home from work she had done a lot of thinking and the more she thought the madder she got.

Anyway, we could hear her ordering Mr. Boyle to go up and make Mr. Irving do something about his "killer" dog. Mr. Boyle kept saying that a lot of dogs kill cats but Mrs. Boyle wouldn't listen. Pretty soon we watched Mr. Boyle walk up to Mr. Irving's and he and Mr. Irving did some talking and Mr. Irving would look at Mr. Boyle and then at Roger and then down at our house. It looked to me as if I might be in trouble but Dad and Mother said what happened really wasn't my or Rex's fault.

After a bit Mr. Boyle and Mr. Irving came down the track and they went in Mr. Boyle's house.

"If Ed keeps pestering Jim, Jim's liable to bust him one," Dad muttered. We found out later Mr. Boyle wasn't "pestering." He was just telling Mr. Irving what happened. After a bit Mr. Irving left the Boyles' and came over to our house. He saw me sitting on my cot and said he was sorry for what happened. He said he forgot to tell me that Roger hated cats. He added that maybe it was best that Rex and I didn't take Roger for any more walks. I asked him if he was going to hurt Roger. He told me no.

Rex and I used to go up and visit Roger often after the cat incident. He seemed to remember Lena Boyle's cat and the good time he had when we took him for a walk. Every time we would go visit him he would dance around and bark and wet and beg us to untie him and take him for a walk again.

But we didn't.

Sometimes we were tempted to but then when we got to thinking back we could see that it just wouldn't be wise. If Lena Boyle were to see us coming down the track again with Roger she probably would faint. And I was pretty sure I knew what Mother would do—she'd tan my pants.

And, anyway, Mr. Irving had said we ought not to.

And at the Western Cooperage, next to Mr. Robinson, Mr. Irving was boss.

18
The Hideaway

Spring always seemed impatient to get started at the Western Cooperage camp. The official debut may have been March 21 on the calendar but in our area almost always the pussy willows were either ready to burst or in full bloom by late February as were daffodils and skunk cabbage.

Skunk cabbage grows in low, moist places and has big greenish yellow leaves with a bright yellow hooded sheath enclosing the yellow flower stalk. Despite its unflattering name, earned because of its skunk-like odor, skunk cabbage was always welcome because it was the first bright color of spring. But it offered more than just a bit of cheery brightness peeking out from the otherwise drab and leafless underbrush. It was a food.

Mother said the early Indians used to prepare the roots as a spring tonic and Fen Johnson said his mother used it once in a while. But I don't think anyone else in camp ever tried to eat it. Mother wouldn't have it in the house and neither would Dad. Fen said it had a peppery taste but I wouldn't know because I didn't like the looks or smell of it as a food.

But bear and elk weren't as finicky. They sought it out in early spring and ate everything, but the roots were the favorite part. We never ate bear meat during skunk cabbage season because its flavor was absorbed by the meat and was so strong it would make you wince.

Mother's favorite early flowers were daffodils. Their golden yellow flowers atop long green stems could be spotted fifty feet away in the underbrush. They grow in clusters from bulbs and everyone in camp seemed to admire and like them, even Mrs. Johnson. She planted some bulbs on Prince's grave and every spring when they bloomed they were so pretty you just knew Prince had to like them.

Among my favorite early spring flowers was the pussy willow. Its gray-white color wasn't much compared with skunk cabbage and daffodils but it was a real fun flower that could be used to make a lot of things. What I liked best was taking a piece of tablet paper, drawing a rail fence, and then with flour and water paste sticking a pussy willow on one of the fence rails. Then you could draw in a head with ears and eyes and a nose and whiskers, add a tail, and you had a kitten sitting on a fence. Mother showed me how to make a kitten on a fence and she said Grandma Snow showed her. On rainy days in pussy willow season I made hundreds of kittens on fences.

What amazed me was that when my friend Rex Gaynor and I started school one of the things our teacher, Miss Della Brown, showed us in early spring was how to make a kitten sitting on a fence. I was never so surprised in my life. I thought for sure Mother must have shown her, but she said no. I thought maybe Grandma Snow had taught her but she said it was her own mother who had taught her. It was just a little disturbing to learn that there were other mothers who knew many of the things my mother knew. I wasn't hurt or jealous or disillusioned by the revelation, but I was surprised. It had always seemed that Mother was the final authority on everything from God and nature to the stars, sky, proper English, good manners, and bedtime stories. That she was the smartest I had no doubt, but the news that some mother I didn't even know might be almost as smart was disquieting.

Miss Brown snatched the furrows from my brow by announcing that Rex and I each had exceptional mothers and if we worked real hard in school she would teach us to read and then we would one day surprise them by reading a real story out of a real book. I asked her if she could help me learn to tell time so Mother and Dad would buy me a real Ingersoll pocket watch such as Dad and the other loggers carried. She said she would. Rex said he wanted to learn, too. After talking with Miss Brown I had to admit again that Mother was right. School and getting an education could be exciting.

I don't know yet what frogs do in winter but I do know that it was usually in February when they began harmonizing again. All of us Churchills loved to snuggle down in bed at night and let the frogs sing us to sleep. A good frog chorus could have Dad snoring within five minutes. I used to try and stay awake just to listen but the soothing chorus of croaking tones never took long to lull me to sleep. The only exception would be when the chorus stopped suddenly, followed by dead silence. That usually meant that some night prowler was in the vicinity. The sudden cessation of sound always erased sleep in the wink of an eyelid. It would be followed by long moments of alertness, straining to hear whatever sound it was the frogs heard. Usually, the chorus would resume as quickly as it had ceased. This meant that whatever danger had been near was now gone and the Western Cooperage camp, its frogs, and its people could relax and go to sleep. Which is what we usually did.

Mother said that if a person listened closely he could usually pick out the leader of a frog chorus. The leader would open with an exploratory note and then one by one others would join in. The frogs in one pond would be joined by voices from another until the night would be filled with sound.

A frog chorus always reminded me of the choir voices in a big church Mother took me to one Sunday when we were in Portland. I had never heard such beautiful voices and harmony and power before. It was beautiful, and liquid, and full of elation. The church also had a big pipe organ that I bet could pop the shingles off the church roof. It was exciting enough to make your flesh tingle and make the hairs on the nape of your neck squirm. I liked church, and I could understand why God liked to go there. I wished we had a church at our camp and I mentioned that to Mother.

Mother said the woods that surrounded our camp was full of little churches. She called them hideaways and said that when we got back to the camp she would show me her special hideaway that even Dad didn't know about. She said it was where she went to talk to God when she had problems, or even when she didn't have problems, and she said it was just as beautiful as the Portland church.

Well, that was the first time Mother had ever told me right out that she talked with God. It seemed to me that God, with a whole world to look after, wouldn't have time to talk to someone like me, or Dad, or Mother. I could understand His talking to a minister, or maybe a man like Mr. Wilson, the President of the United States, but not to us almost lost in a remote Coast Range logging camp. I thought perhaps someone like Daddy O'Hoyt or Uncle Marsh had played a trick on her and talked to her and she thought it was God.

She said no matter where a person went God was there—even if he climbed down inside a deep hole, or up to the top of Saddle Mountain, or even up to the moon. And, she said, God had time for everyone and everything from the tiniest bug in an old piece of rotted wood to me.

She said it was impossible for anyone to play a trick on you when you were talking with God because God didn't talk out loud like people do. She said when you talked with God you just seemed to know what He said without hearing anything. She said God's talk was an inside good feeling like when you love somebody a whole lot. It was all I could do to wait to see Mother's hideaway.

It was a late spring afternoon shortly after we returned to the camp from Portland that Mother took me to her secret woods spot. We walked up the railroad track past the machine shop and Mr. Bramble's office, up past the cookhouse and the bunk-houses on railroad trucks, which was where the men on the rail-road section crew were housed.

We walked on up past the powder house, a medium-sized structure built of heavy wooden planks with a heavy plank door that was always kept locked. It was here that the company stored its dynamite, caps, and fuse. It was kind of a dangerous spot and Dad and Mother always warned me not to play in that area. I never heard of a powder house blowing up, but if ours ever had, it would have taken the section crew bunkhouses and probably some other buildings with it.

Mother's special spot was a half mile or so beyond our camp and toward Camp 2. It wasn't too far from the gravel pit where Mr. Alex Carlson's steam shovel would sometimes load whole trains of rock for railroad ballast. Sometimes when the company was building a lot of railroad and Mr. Carlson's steam shovel was busy, Mrs. Carlson, Mother, and I would walk up and watch. We would take a lunch and spend most of the day there. If Mr. Robinson or Mr. Irving wasn't around Mr. Carlson would sometimes let me climb up into the steam shovel cab with him and watch him operate the levers.

One of the most exciting times would be when the crew would set off a dynamite blast to break up more rock from the cliff that was the source of all the Western Cooperage Company's railroad ballast. When it was time to blast, Mr. Carlson would shut down his machine and lead Mrs. Carlson, Mother, and me down the tracks a safe distance from the rock pit. The powder man would set the charge, light the fuse, then yell, "Fire in the hole," several times so as to warn anyone headed that way. After that everything was quiet for a minute or two as we waited for the burning powder in the fuse to reach the cap, which would set off the charge. Sometimes I would be sweating with the excitement of waiting for the blast. The waiting period always made Mother nervous. She would grip my hand until it hurt and her body would be tense as a steel spring.

When the blast would finally let go it was never as loud as I had expected because it was so deep in the face of the rock cliff it was muffled. But it would shake the earth like some giant creature and a great cloud of powder smoke and dust would mark the spot of the gravel pit. Mr. Carlson always made us wait a few minutes after the blast to make certain all the dynamite had exploded at the same time. After that we would hurry back to the pit and Mr. Carlson's steam shovel to see what had happened. I always expected to see Mr. Carlson's steam shovel either buried in rock or pelted to pieces by flying rock from the explosion, but it always seemed to survive. Now and then it would get a dent or a broken window from a stray piece of flying rock but the charge was concentrated deep in the cliff wall, so not much rock would fly free in the air.

It was just before we got to the gravel pit that Mother turned from the railroad track and headed into the woods. We followed a dim path that I was sure Mother had made and all of a sudden we were standing in a tiny garden spot where the ground was covered with moss and ferns. Slanting pillars of sunshine came bursting through the overhanging tops of trees and floodlighted the ground with a golden sheen.

Mother stood very still for a long moment as though absorbing each and every detail of the vision. Finally, motioning me to follow, she stepped toward an old moss-covered windfall.

"This is where I talk to God," she said, kneeling and placing her elbows on the windfall. "You can come here and talk to Him, too, or maybe you would rather find your own hideaway."

"I like yours," I said, kneeling beside her. It was so clean, peaceful, and pretty that without anyone telling you, you just knew God was there. Mother's hideaway was even better than the big church in Portland. It didn't have the vibrating sounds of the organ or the tutored harmony of the choir, but it had the friendly chattery sounds of nearby Klaskanine Creek and the animated voices of God's own birds. It was all so gentle and reverent I wanted to pray but first I wanted to hear Mother talk with God.

With my hand in hers we bowed our heads and Mother tried to say something but she wasn't doing very well. I think she was used to being alone when talking with God and my being there distracted her. She finally just said a few neighborly things to God: things like asking God to forgive Mrs. Johnson and her swearing, to watch over Dad and me and all the other people in camp, and to help her to be an understanding wife and mother, and the news that maybe I would be coming here sometimes. She then told me to go ahead and say something.

Well, I had never gotten right down on my knees to talk to God, except at bedtime beside my cot. This was different. In the first place it was daylight. And it was outside. Words just wouldn't seem to come. I heard a limb crack beyond the little clearing and I wondered if God had stepped on it, or if someone was spying on us, or if maybe it was a deer or a bear. I began getting uneasy.

Mother said not to be afraid, that God was with us. She said she didn't think that cracking sound was God stepping on a limb. That made me even more nervous because if it wasn't God, then what was it? If God really was with us I kind of wished He would say something out loud or make Himself visible so I would know for sure He was there.

Mother again urged me to talk to God. "Just imagine you are talking to me or your father, or Rex Gaynor," she said, trying to encourage me. "God will understand."

Well, I shut my eyes real tight and tried to imagine I was talking with Dad. I chose Dad because he was big and strong and, like God, wasn't afraid of anything, except maybe garter snakes, which could send him leaping straight up if he happened to look down and was about to step on one. Mother used to laugh and could never understand how a grown man who could walk a woods trail in the middle of the night and never even think about a cougar or a bear could let a little garter snake upset him.

Dad wasn't really afraid of snakes. It was that he didn't like them and, besides, they always seemed to slither into view so unexpectedly they tended to startle people.

Even with my eyes shut and trying to imagine I was talking to Dad I couldn't think of anything important to say to God, so I finally told Him that I wished every little boy in the world had a mother like mine.

After that I kept my head bowed and my eyes closed waiting for Mother to say good-by to God and dismiss us. But she just stayed there, kneeling and saying nothing. I finally took a peek and she was crying. I could tell because tears were running down her cheek and dribbling from her chin. I was stunned. I knew I must have said something bad to God to make her cry but I couldn't, for the life of me, think what it could have been.

I touched her arm and told her I was sorry I made her cry and that I wouldn't talk to God any more.

"No, no, no," she sobbed, grabbing me in her arms and holding me so tight I could hardly breathe. "That was beautiful," she said, "the most beautiful prayer I have ever heard." She said God must have liked it, too, and I must never stop talking to Him. I couldn't believe that it had been all that good but if Mother and God were pleased with it, then it must have been fairly good.

I had to admit to Mother that I didn't mind talking to God but that it wasn't much fun talking to someone you couldn't see and who never talked back. Mother said a person just had to believe. You had to just know that God was there and that He was listening.

All that summer Mother and I would walk up to our hideaway at least once a week for talks with God and between us. She said that when we were at our hideaway I could tell her anything I wanted and it would be just between us three—me, God, and her. Dad could come, too, and sometimes he would, but most of the times we went to our hideaway Dad was at work. Lots of times I told Mother things in our hideaway that I wouldn't have dared tell her had we been home or for a walk. I guess having God there helped. I was pretty certain He wouldn't let Mother give me a spanking as long as He was around. And He didn't.

Some of the things I told her upset her a little and she would caution me. But she was careful not to scold or break her promise to keep what I told her a secret.

She was a little disturbed when I told her Rex Gaynor and I liked to take off our clothes in the woods and play Indian. Or when I told her Jake Johnson was teaching me how to smoke. Or about peeking through the knotholes in the girls' outhouse at school. Or seeing one of the Peets girls naked. I didn't tell her about some of the other things. They were a little too embarrassing to talk about to your mother, or even God.

Our hideaway brought me a lot closer to Mother and to God. After a while, any time I went to the hideaway I could almost see God sitting on that old moss-covered log waiting for me. You just knew He was there.

And many times, when we kids were playing, I would duck into our hideaway real quick just to say hello to God so He would know I hadn't forgotten Him.

19
From Here to Forever

The summer before Mr. Robinson moved Dad from his rigging job in the woods to the machine shop, we lived at a logging camp called Little Big Creek.

It was five miles from our camp to Little Big Creek and to get there you followed the Western Cooperage railroad almost to Camp 2. Instead of going to Camp 2 you took a branch line up the north side of Klaskanine Creek, across from Camp 2, then doubled back along the north ridge of what we called Bear Mountain. Little Big Creek was in the vicinity of where we went to watch the eclipse of the sun. The logs from Little Big Creek were loaded on Western Cooperage rail cars and hauled over the Western Cooperage line to the log dump at Olney.

I didn't much like Little Big Creek and it was lonely for Mother, too. All of her friends were at the Western Cooperage headquarters camp, a long five-mile hike by railroad track. The five-mile one-way hike wasn't so bad but the country was big and rather wild, and extremely rough. The jumble of steep slopes, high ridges, and deep canyons resulted in a number of high trestles on the railroad line. Mother didn't like heights and even to walk across a medium-high trestle she had to steel herself. The trick was to keep your eyes on the ties a few feet ahead of where you were stepping. But Mother always stared straight down at her feet and by doing that she would be looking between the ties to the ground, which on a couple of trestles was ninety feet down.

If a person looked down, it was easy to get dizzy and panicky. Besides, Mother was always afraid a log train would come along and catch her in the middle of a trestle. I showed her how to get down on her knees and lay one ear against the top of a track rail. The sounds of a train on the track would telegraph along the rails and you could hear it that way long before you could hear it by cupping your ear and listening the usual way. If you couldn't hear any train sounds through a track rail you had time to walk any trestle on the Western Cooperage railroad, if you walked at a fair pace. I tried to tell Mother that but although she would nod she was never really convinced.

One time I spent most of an afternoon trying to get her to cross a long and rather high trestle. Finally, to demonstrate how easy it was, and safe, I put my ear to a rail to check on train sounds and hearing none stood up and raced across the trestle like the wind. We kids ran across trestles all the time. It was kind of an exciting game and lots of fun. I don't think it took me a half minute to get across, a time span that provided an ample safety margin even if a train did happen to sneak up on a person.

When I got to the other side and looked back, Mother was waving her arms and shouting. I was too far away to hear what she was saying but I judged she was excited about something. Maybe she had seen a bear in the canyon, or wanted me to hurry back. I decided she wanted me back in a hurry. I checked the rail sounds again and, hearing nothing, hurried back to the other side.

On the return I ran almost as hard as I could go. The railroad ties, spaced about eight or ten inches apart on trestles, fairly flew under my feet. It was almost like racing along the edge of a cloud. My hair flew, I could feel the blood beating through my body, and my eyes were glued to the ties a few feet ahead of where my feet were landing.

When I got to the other side I pulled up, panting, in front of Mother. I was expecting at least a little praise for my feat and the agility and control I had demonstrated. Instead I got a sweeping embrace and a flood of kisses, and then a tongue-lashing.

It seemed that when I was on the other side and Mother was waving her arms and yelling she was trying to tell me not to run on the trestle. Instead of being happy and pleased she had been about to faint. Dad came to my rescue that night at supper. Dad was used to railroad trestles and could walk across one with his eyes shut. He wasn't much impressed with my running across one. He had done the same thing hundreds of times, he told Mother. And after all, I was no longer a little boy. I was almost eight.

"But what if he should stumble?" exploded Mother.

"He'd bang his face into the ties and probably get a scratched knee and hands," shrugged Dad.

"He could fall between the ties and be killed," insisted Mother, her voice almost a shout.

"Nonsense," declared Dad, "the ties are too close together. He couldn't fall through."

"But he could roll over the side," snapped Mother.

Dad hadn't thought of that possibility. A compromise was reached, with Dad's help. I could trot across a trestle when it was necessary to keep up with the other kids, but no more racing and hard running.

"When you can, it is best to do as your mother wants, walk," said Dad.

After the trestle incident I had a hard time getting Mother to walk across any trestle, even fairly low ones. She said whenever she got out on a trestle she would start thinking of me and the way I flew across that high one. The thought of what might have happened to me would get her so nervous and on edge she couldn't keep her eyes and mind on what she was supposed to be doing.

Because of the trestles we would have to cross, Mother and I never walked the railroad track from Little Big Creek to the Western Cooperage headquarters camp. There was also a woods trail that cut over Bear Mountain. By trail the distance was only about a mile and a half, but Mother would have none of that. I felt the same way about the trail. Loggers who used it often reported seeing bear or cougar. Dad said most of those reports were just stories. It didn't matter. Mother was convinced and so was I.

The only way left to get from Little Big Creek to our old camp, then, was by log train. A Western Cooperage locomotive brought up empty cars and hauled out the loaded cars once a day, usually in the afternoon. Taking it to the headquarters camp meant Mother and I would have to stay overnight with someone and there weren't many extra beds in logging camp homes. Our house was there and most of our furniture was still in it but Mother and Dad's bed and my sleeping cot were now at Little Big Creek.

I just couldn't learn to like Little Big Creek, even though I knew it was only temporary and we would be back at the Western Cooperage camp in time for me to go to school in the fall. It was a lonely camp. There were only a few families and no kids my age except a girl, and she wasn't much fun. We undressed and played Indian sometimes but she didn't know as much about being an Indian as Rex Gaynor did. Anyway, undressing in front of her was kind of embarrassing. I always had the feeling Mother wouldn't approve if she knew. And the girl's mother probably wouldn't like it, either.

One thing I did like about living at Little Big Creek, though, was its altitude. The ridge the camp was on must have been 2,000 feet or more in height and from our front steps I could look across the California Barrel basin toward Wickiup Mountain and see Big Creek log trains going back and forth between camps and woods. The main Big Creek operation was across the basin and covered a huge area of the Big Creek watershed. The Big Creek Logging Company main-line railroad, spur lines, and camps reached from the Columbia River deep into the Coast Range, and almost into the Nehalem Valley near Jewell. Our Little Big Creek camp was set up by the main Big Creek company to log a small block of timber bordering Western Cooperage holdings. It was too small to be worth building a railroad line to, especially when the Western Cooperage already had a railroad into the area. So the parent Big Creek company decided to log it but haul the logs out on the Western Cooperage railroad.

In addition to Wickiup Mountain we could see from Little Big Creek other spots such as Saddle Mountain, sort of to the south of us, and Fog Mountain (now called Elk Mountain) to the northeast of us. To the west on a clear day you could see the Pacific Ocean, seventeen or so air miles distant. North and east of Fog Mountain was Nicolai Mountain. None of these was a big snow-capped mountain like Mount Hood, up near Portland, or Mount St. Helens and Mount Adams over in Washington State, but they were rugged, and big, and loaded with timber. Saddle Mountain was the highest, almost 3,300 feet. Nicolai was a little over 3,000 feet and Wickiup Mountain was almost 2,800 feet.

I liked mountains. They reminded me of Dad—big, strong, solid, and not afraid of anything. Mother said mountains were good because they got you up to where you see out over things. I liked the woods but down on the ground surrounded by big Douglas fir and hemlock trees a body couldn't really see much. You couldn't see the Pacific Ocean from the Western Cooperage headquarters camp because the camp was down in a canyon and surrounded by forest. But from the top of Bear Mountain, which stood there with its feet almost in the camp, you could see the ocean and even Astoria.

There was a powerful lot of country surrounding the Western

Cooperage and Little Big Creek camps. It didn't seem especially far across the California Barrel basin but by line of sight it was two miles or so. Now, two miles isn't very far and Dad and Mother and I used to walk that far lots of times on our Sunday afternoon walks. But the basin was full of standing timber and it was all old, thick, and virgin except where the California Barrel Logging Company was beginning to work into it on the western edge.

Well, one night when Dad came home from work he announced at supper that he was going to have to go to bed early and get up early. When Mother asked why, he said he had to walk over to the Big Creek logging operation on the other side of the basin and pick up a spare part for a donkey engine and bring it back in time for the donkey engine crew to install it and be ready to log by starting time in the morning.

"You have to walk over there and back through the woods, at night?" Mother gasped. Dad nodded. I was petrified. This very day while playing down the railroad track from our house I had heard a terrible roaring and caterwauling out of sight down the canyon from the railroad tracks. I was certain it was two bears fighting but I was too frightened to walk to the edge and find out. Instead I raced for home, my fear-inspired feet and legs leaping three ties at a time as I tore up the track for home.

And now here was Dad telling us he was going to hike right into that very same area in the middle of the night with only a dim trail and the light of a kerosene lantern to guide him. I told him what I had heard that very day. Then I began to cry. Mother was filled with apprehension and dread.

"Why do you have to walk?" she wanted to know. "Why can't they send word to Astoria and have the part sent out by the regular mail and freight route to the Western Cooperage and then by log train up here?"

Dad said that would be a waste of time, that they would have the spare part ready for him where we could see them logging so he could turn around and come right back. This way the company would lose no logging time. Having it shipped out from Astoria might take two or three days.

I tell you that was a mighty lonely night for Mother and me at Little Big Creek. We all went to bed right after supper. Dad set the alarm clock for midnight and when the alarm went off we all got up. Dad dressed but Mother and I stayed in our night clothes with robes thrown around us. Mother fixed Dad a big breakfast of mush, bacon and eggs, toast, and coffee. He seemed as jolly as though it were 6 A.M. and he were merely getting up at the routine time on a routine workday.

While Dad ate the breakfast Mother had prepared she made him a sandwich that he could tuck in his coat pocket and produced a couple of fresh oranges for the other pocket. When everything was ready Dad went outside, sat on the steps, and laced on his calk shoes. Mother left the door open so he could see. I went outside in my robe and pajamas. It wasn't cold and there were a lot of stars in the sky but beyond the light of our house lamp the outside looked black and mighty scary. Again I started to cry. I just knew that Dad might never come back, that a hungry cougar could easily track him on that lonely trail, or he could meet up with a bear, or maybe even a timber wolf, because some loggers had reported seeing wolves on occasion.

When I started crying, that got Mother to crying. Dad must have been about ready to give the whole thing up and go back to bed. But he didn't. He tried to be patient and sympathetic but it was hard to do because he was in a hurry and in his own mind could see no earthly reason for anyone to be fearful of a midnight hike of two miles across the California Barrel basin and then back.

He checked his lantern to make sure it had plenty of kerosene. He lit it and adjusted the wick for a clear, bright flame. He gave Mother a hearty hug and a kiss and told her to go back to bed "and don't worry. I'll be back before you wake up." He wanted to know if I would like to walk down our steps to the railroad track with him, and carry his lantern. I said I would. It felt good to carry a big, grownup's lantern and help get Dad started. When we got to the railroad track Dad took the lantern, gave me a pat on the head, and asked me to take care of Mother until he got back. Then he headed off into the night down the track toward the spot where the basin trail swung up out of the canyon and met the railroad.

I ran back up the steps and stood beside Mother. We watched the little circle of lantern light grow smaller and smaller. Then it turned left and disappeared over the edge of the canyon. I could feel Mother's body trembling. I kept hoping the speck of light would reappear, that Dad would discover he had forgotten something and have to come back. I watched and watched but the light didn't reappear. I could feel my throat tightening and tears starting to gather. I wanted to let everything go and bust out in a real little-boy cry. But I couldn't. Dad had asked me to watch over Mother.

Mother and I tried to go back to bed and sleep as Dad had suggested but it was no use. We went back to bed but we couldn't sleep. I crawled in under the covers with her but all we did was roll and toss until we finally got up. I thought it must be almost five o'clock, the hour Dad expected to be back. Mother must have felt the same because she struck a match and lighted the lamp. It was 1:30 A.M. Dad had only been gone a half hour.

Mother got out my *Burgess Bird Book for Children*, placed the lamp on a shelf near the bed, propped her head up with an extra pillow, and began to read. She told me later she chose the bird book to get both our minds off animals. I remember Mother reading about Jenny Wren and Sammy Jay and then the next moment I was sitting straight up in bed and there was Dad's booming voice shaking the house with: "Wake up, wake up. Are you two going to sleep all day?"

Mother bounded out of bed and into Dad's arms. The lamp was still burning. She had read us both to sleep.

"What time is it?" I asked.

"Half past five and the sun's been up for over an hour," Dad shouted, picking me up and tucking me under his arm as though I were a sack of flour.

On the kitchen table there was a small piece of shiny metal with threaded studs and some grooves.

"What on earth is that?" asked Mother, pointing to the piece of metal on the table.

"That's the donkey engine part I went after," said Dad.

"Do you mean to tell me the company sent you out in the middle of the night for *that?*" gasped Mother.

"A donkey engine won't run without it," shrugged Dad.

One day I told Mother I was tired of playing with a girl and wished we could go down to our old camp so I could see Rex Gaynor and the other kids who were my friends. She said she would ask Mr. Mullins, the Little Big Creek superintendent, if we could ride down and back with him on some of his trips.

Mr. Mullins was a young redheaded fellow who could rip off cuss words faster than Mrs. Johnson. One time when he was in St. Mary's Hospital in Astoria to have his appendix out, he swore so much when he was coming out from under the ether his doctor told him about it. Mr. Mullins was so embarrassed that when he left the hospital he went down to the Hoefler Candy Company and bought the biggest box of chocolate candy he could buy and took it up to the sisters with his apologies.

The sisters were real jolly about it and told Mr. Mullins he needn't have worried because they had all crammed cotton in their ears and never heard a word he said. Mr. Mullins used to tell that story on himself. He said if he ever had to have another operation he would insist the doctor tape up his mouth.

Mr. Mullins went by the name of Red. He had a speeder, a gasoline-powered small railroad errand car used by officials and section crews. The engine of a speeder is small and noisy but it can send the little four-wheel car scooting along the rails like a jack rabbit. All railroad section crews use speeders.

Mother asked Mr. Mullins if she and I could ride with him

sometime on one of his trips to the Western Cooperage head-quarters camp. He said we could go that very day because he was leaving in an hour and would be at our old camp for a couple of hours. Mother said we would be ready. He stopped the speeder right in front of our house and all we had to do was walk down the steps and get on.

Mr. Mullins' speeder didn't have a roof or a windshield like some speeders but it had handholds and Mr. Mullins told us to hang on tight. The engine was right under where we sat. Mr. Mullins opened the throttle as soon as we got settled and within seconds the wind was tearing at my hair. Mother had one of the handholds in a death grip with one hand and was clutching her hat with the other. Mr. Mullins had his red felt logging hat pulled down tight on his head. The loose folds of his hickory-weave shirt flapped like crow's wings in the wind.

In no time at all I noticed that the clicks of the speeder's wheels on rail joints were coming so fast I could hardly keep up trying to count them. I wanted to tell Mr. Mullins to slow down but it was almost impossible to talk because the moment you would open your mouth the wind would grab words and breath right out of it.

The little speeder was rocking from side to side as it raced through deep cuts, around curves, and across trestles. When we hit some of those high trestles Mother was afraid to walk across we were over them before you could say Kaiser Bill went up the hill to take a look at France.

When we came down the grade across the canyon from Camp 2 my eyes were so wind-burned everything was a blur. Mr. Carlson's steam shovel at the gravel pit shot by so fast I wouldn't have had time to see him if he had been standing right by the railroad track. Mother's and my hideaway spot was behind us before I knew it.

Mr. Mullins eased up on the throttle and began gently touching the brake pedal a quarter of a mile before we arrived at the headquarters camp. We pulled to a stop right in front of the office walk and Mr. Mullins had his pocket watch in his hand.

"Jumpin' Jesus, we did it," he shouted.

"Did what?" asked Mother, still clutching the handhold with one hand and her hat with the other.

"Made it down here from our camp in five minutes. That's sixty miles an hour," he whooped. "The good Lord was with us."

"I'll be eternally grateful to Him for that," sighed Mother, easing herself from the car and holding on to it for support while she steadied her nerves and got her breathing under control.

Leaving Mr. Mullins and his speed record, we walked down the track to Aunt Blanche's house. Mother was grateful for a steaming hot cup of coffee and a chair. I got some hot cocoa and cookies. Mother told Aunt Blanche about our wild ride with Mr. Mullins. Aunt Blanche said Mr. Mullins was a wild man and shouldn't be allowed to run a speeder on any railroad or drive an automobile anyplace but a vacant farm pasture. Mother was uneasy about the ride back but Aunt Blanche reminded her that that was all uphill and Mr. Mullins' speeder just wasn't built for speed on steep railroad grades.

After my cocoa and cookies I hunted up Rex Gaynor and we explored Klaskanine Creek and played Indian until Mother called and it was time to go back to Little Big Creek.

On the way back Aunt Blanche was right. Mr. Mullins made pretty good time but it took about four times as long going as it did coming. The comical part was that at the slower speed Mother shut her eyes and gripped both handholds every time we would come to a high trestle. On the way down she was so busy hanging on to her hat and gasping for breath she didn't even think about them.

For several weeks after our fast ride, any time Mr. Mullins was going down to the headquarters camp he would stop in front of our house and yell. Mother said no so many times he finally stopped asking. But ours was the fastest trip. Mr. Mullins never hit a mile a minute again. He said the extra weight of Mother and me helped hold the car to the rails and enabled him to take curves just enough faster to make that record.

From that time on, when Mother and I went down to the headquarters camp we rode the log train in the cab of Mr. Cox's locomotive. We would have to stay all night but Aunt Blanche and Uncle Marsh made room for us. Mother and Aunt Blanche slept in the bed and Uncle Marsh and I slept on the floor.

On a clear night at the Western Cooperage or Little Big Creek camps, or most any logging camp, you could look up at the sky and seem to see forever. Mother said that being on any high spot on a clear summer's night had to be almost like being in heaven and I guess she was right.

During the day our camps were an ugly scar on the breast of the earth. For the most part they consisted of unpainted, weatherworn buildings of rough-cut lumber that were almost the color of the dead snags and gloomy-looking stumps.

But at night the soft glow of a half or full moon, or the almost phosphoric glimmer of a billion stars, seemed to mellow the harshness of the daylight image and bring peace and contentment not only to the camp and the land, but to the people.

Sometimes on a clear summer's night Mother would spread blankets under the clotheslines, and with pillows under our heads we would look up at the stars. Mostly it was just the two of us but once in a while she could talk Dad into doing it. But he wasn't much fun. Almost as soon as his head would hit the pillow he would end up going to sleep and snoring. One night, as a joke, Mother said not to awaken him when we went in the house to go to bed. We didn't and Dad slept out there under the stars most of the night. He didn't wake up until the Johnsons' new dog, Shotgun, came by, sniffed, and wet on him. Jake said that was why they named him Shotgun, he could put more pee on a target than a shotgun had pellets. Dad woke up with a bellow and that gave poor Shotgun such a start he unloaded another full round on Dad before leaping clear of Dad's feet and crashing for home through the underbrush, kiyiiiing and barking.

Mother didn't tell Dad, but afterward she told me that she didn't think Dad had kicked Shotgun and hurt him. She said she was quite sure Shotgun's hollering was just his way of laughing.

Well, Dad wasn't laughing. He came storming into the house and wanted to know what Mother meant by letting him sleep outside all night. Mother told him to go outside and change clothes. She said he smelled like dog wet, and he did. That made Dad so angry he flipped back the covers and crawled right in beside Mother, dog wet and all. Mother popped out of bed as though Dad were a bee and squeezed in with me on my cot. She was almost pushing me out on the floor, so I got up and got in the big bed with Dad.

I don't know exactly what happened later on that night but when I awoke next morning I was back in my cot and Dad and Mother were back in their big bed.

As I've said before—grownups are sure hard to figure out.

Getting back to the stars. Mother didn't know an awful lot about the moon and the stars but she read a lot and she often saved clippings and articles for later reference and reading. She said when we looked at the black spots in the sky between stars we were looking into forever, that there was no end. Well, I couldn't quite believe that. Everything I had ever seen or heard of had an end. A tree had a top and a bottom; I had been to the end of the Western Cooperage railroad; the main line of a steam donkey engine that yarded in logs had an end. I told Mother my thoughts. I couldn't imagine God making something and forgetting to put an end on it.

That seemed to intrigue Mother. She said maybe I was right. Anyway, she said, each person should have his own ideas and do his own thinking and she was proud that I had expressed my views and that my views didn't always agree with hers.

She had another idea. She said to her mind when you got to the very last star in the universe everything beyond that was heaven. And there was no end to heaven. Mother was awfully smart. If God was going to leave off some ends it sure enough would be when He built heaven.

One night as Mother and I were outside on our blankets looking up at the sky Mother suggested we make up a word to describe what we were seeing. I tried and tried to think of a word but none would come to mind, so I finally said, "God."

Mother thought and thought, and thought some more. Finally, she said she was going to have to give up.

"I think you picked the best word, the exactly right word, Samuel," she said. "The only word that could possibly express what we are looking at tonight is GOD." I guess that was just about the happiest moment in my whole life.

I reached over and took her hand. "I love you," I said, "I love you more than anybody in the whole world."

She leaned over to kiss me and there was a wet spot on her cheek. "What a lucky woman I am," she said, "to be living here with you, and God, and your father."

It made me all warm inside to hear her say that. I don't know why, but I had wet spots on my cheeks, too.

20
Long Journey Home

When Dad finished his summer work at Little Big Creek we returned to the Western Cooperage headquarters camp and our house that was bigger and more comfortable.

Mother was happy to be back where there were more women and no high trestles to worry about. I was pleased to be back with all my friends.

The only one not really happy was Dad. Mr. Robinson had moved him from the woods to the machine shop and he was having a hard time getting used to it. He missed the smell of fresh-cut timber, the feel of calks digging into wood, the whiplashing sounds of steel cables, and the constant chatter of steam donkey whistles and the shouts and curses of straining, sweating men.

"He's as edgy as a he bear settin' in a pan of hot pitch," Daddy O'Hoyt told Mother.

"Give him a little time," suggested Mother. "When the winter rains come and it's cold and miserable in the woods he'll be happy to have a roof over his head." And that was the way it turned out. Working in the machine shop, Dad didn't have to get up so early in the morning and he could come home for a hot lunch instead of eating cold sandwiches out of a lunch bucket. And as Mother had predicted, when the winter storms came and the rains came pounding down Dad often remarked how good it felt not to have water running down the back of his neck.

But the machine shop had other things in its favor. When the logging operations had to close down because of storms, holiday periods, or poor log prices the machine shop usually kept right on working because it was during shutdowns that repair and maintenance work on locomotives, cars, and logging machines was done. This meant that shop crews got in a lot more working hours each year than woods crews. A lot of that extra money went into the bank for me as a fund for my college education.

I wasn't too concerned about college. My first love was still Mr. Casey's Shay No. 2. If I couldn't be a locomotive engineer I would settle for being a fireman on one of those big fire trucks such as they had in Astoria and Portland; or maybe a policeman, or even some kind of a civil engineer who built railroad lines, and laid out camps and designed trestles. But best of all would be being a locomotive engineer.

Mother and Dad didn't say much any more but I could feel them pressing for civil engineering and using that as a means to work in a logging camp, if logging turned out to be what I really wanted to be involved in.

The Western Cooperage Company prospered and the timber industry in general boomed during World War I but after the war things started easing down and the economy faded into what Mother and Dad termed a depression. Log prices began dropping, the company began tightening its belt. It was during this period that Mr. Robinson moved Dad from the woods to the machine shop.

This readjustment period continued from the latter part of 1919 into 1920 and 1921. There were shutdowns when nothing but the machine shop was operating. As the shutdowns became more numerous even the machine shop would stop working.

During these periods of idleness, as far as paydays were concerned, Dad and Mother saw to it that we all kept busy. Dad kept busy sawing and cutting wood. During one shutdown he built an addition to our woodshed. I helped him cut down and peel young trees for the framework of the walls and rafters for the roof. After that he found an old cedar tree that had been blown down by some forgotten storm. In the camp we called such trees windfalls. With a crosscut saw Dad sawed a portion of the fallen tree into blocks about three feet long. With a special tool called a froe, an instrument like a cleaver with a handle perpendicular to the blade, we split the blocks into heavy shingle-like boards called shakes. We lugged the shakes on our backs out of the woods and Dad nailed them to the peeled-pole frame studdings to make the sides of the addition. More shakes were used to cover the roof.

During the summer Mother canned several hundred jars of fruit and vegetables, including wild blackberries, which grew in abundance in logged-off areas that now surrounded the camp. Nature also provided us with red and blue wild huckleberries for a fruit dish, pies, and fresh eating. There were lots of red elderberries for wine, if you wanted a beverage, or jelly. There were apples in unlimited quantities from abandoned pioneer orchards that were left untended along the railroad track near Olney. We called them sweet apples and they were delicious fresh and made excellent apple sauce and dandy pies. Mother canned dozens of quarts of apple sauce.

There were all the other foods such as venison, bear meat, fish, grouse, and other birds, all there for the taking.

Actually, if there was to be a depression the Western Cooperage was about as comfortable a place to sit one out as you can imagine. The company provided worker houses, so there was no rent or taxes. We depended upon kerosene lamps for light and the only telephone was in the company office. And during the summer, spring, and fall we were virtually surrounded by foods that nature provided.

But the depression did make changes. A number of old familiar faces began disappearing. The Cox family moved, as did the Peetses, the Boyles, Aunt Blanche and Uncle Marsh, the Gaynors, the Ziaks, and others. Mr. and Mrs. Robinson left. It was Mr. Robinson's job Mr. Smith and other company officials wanted Dad to take, but he wouldn't. The new superintendent was Mr. Steve Ridley. He was not a big man but he was nice. His wife was bigger than he was but she was friendly and she and Mother became close friends. She was like Mother: she liked to read and discuss things.

Finally, Mr. and Mrs. Casey were gone and so was Mr. Jim Irving. Worst of all, Mr. Casey's No. 2 Shay was gone. The company sold it and bought a bigger, heavier rod engine. The new engine carried No. 4 on its side and we called it the Four-Spot. I didn't like it at all when Shay No. 1 came towing it into camp. They parked it on a siding by the machine shop and a crew, including a new engineer, named Mr. Tate, began getting it ready to steam up and operate. Mr. and Mrs. Tate and their sons, Howard and Frank, moved in across the tracks from us into the old Eddie and Lena Boyle house. One Tate boy, Frank, was a fireman and he would fire the new engine for his dad. Howard was four grades ahead of me in school. He didn't care much about school. He said he had run a locomotive and he was going to be an engineer just like his dad.

I didn't like Mr. Tate at first because he took Mr. Casey's job but Mother liked him. She said he was an excellent cribbage player. And I still didn't like the No. 4 rod engine. But the first time I saw it dragging a long string of empties up the grade into camp I changed my mind. Old No. 4 was bellowing like one of those storybook dragons. Black smoke boiled out of its stack. And when it whistled for the county road crossing it was a whole new world. Even Mother came outside to watch. No. 4 had the most beautiful whistle I have ever heard. When Mr. Tate blew it, it just rolled back and forth along the canyon slopes that walled in our camp, in a thunderhead of sound and music. And when No. 4 thundered past our house Mr. Tate gave another blast from its whistle and Frank Tate rang its bell. Mr. Tate stood at the cab window with his hand on the throttle. He waved and grinned and Mother and I waved back. Mr. Tate always stood up when he was running No. 4. He never used the engineer's seat. I asked him why. He said No. 4 was a lot of locomotive and he just felt better standing up.

"No. 4 reminds me of your father," Mother used to say. "It is so big and strong. And when it speaks it speaks with authority."

The Johnsons were still in camp. Mrs. Johnson didn't seem to fret much about the depression. She said it had its points and one of them was that Sharkey Bramble was gone. The new head of the office was a Mr. Hughes, who was sent down from the Portland office.

The depression began to ease but the Western Cooperage still wasn't logging. The machine shop was running and that meant Dad had a job, but that was because the company was hauling logs over its railroad for other companies such as the California Barrel, Potter and Chester, and a couple of others. That was one reason it bought No. 4: it needed a heavier, more powerful locomotive to do the job.

There was talk that the old Western Cooperage Company was actually having money troubles, and rumors that it was going to reorganize and become a new company. In a year or so it did. It became the Tidewater Timber Company. It rebuilt the old Western Cooperage railroad, bought several locomotives even bigger than No. 4, and rebuilt the old machine shop into a bigger, more modern one. Dad was still there but I was having problems.

It was the spring of 1922 and Howard Tate and I were the only two pupils in the Western Cooperage school. The problem was that at the end of the school year in May, Howard would graduate. I was only in the fourth grade.

"The board will have to continue the school for Samuel," Mother insisted to Dad. Dad wasn't so sure, even though Mother was still the board's clerk and prepared to argue my case right up to the county school superintendent in Astoria. But she didn't.

She tried to convince the Western Cooperage board but the members, although sympathetic and sorry, had their minds made up. Their conclusion: "Caroline, we aren't going to hire a teacher at one hundred dollars a month just to teach Samuel."

"What will we do?" Mother asked Dad that evening after the board meeting.

Dad said there was only one thing we could do. He would stay at the camp and Mother and I would move into town, either Astoria or the nearby beach resort community of Seaside, so that I could continue my education.

Mother said she would not do that. Dad said she would. And she did. But leaving our old Western Cooperage camp was a sad moment and I'll never forget it. Mother sobbed and carried on something fierce. I bawled and said I wanted one more ride in the cab of No. 4 with Mr. Tate before I left.

Mr. Tate gave me a quick ride from the machine shop siding down to the county road crossing and back. As we passed our house on the way back to the siding Mr. Tate opened old No. 4's throttle and told me to grab the whistle cord and pull. I did and you never heard a more beautiful sound, even out of a moving picture house pipe organ. Dad and Mother stood on our front porch, waving. It was a memorable moment for all of us because three people and a company—Mr. Tate and his son Frank, who was the locomotive's fireman; Mr. Ernest Towne, a brakeman; and the Western Cooperage Company—saw fit to satisfy the whim of a small boy. It was conclusive evidence of the inherent goodness in man, Mother observed that night at supper.

I never did really get to run a Western Cooperage locomotive. But I did get to sit on the engineer's seat, lean my head out the cab window, and blow the whistle. Mother said that was a lot more than most boys my age ever get to do. I guess she was right because at the time I was ten going on eleven but the memories of that moment are among the most exciting of my life.

In the fall of that same year (1922) Mother and I moved from the camp to Seaside so I could continue school. An association of almost eleven years was about to be broken.

On the day before Billy Deeds was to come by and pick up our stuff Mother and I spent a leisurely day saying good-by to the things and the people we had become so familiar with at the camp. We took off our shoes and stockings and dipped our feet in the icy waters of Klaskanine Creek. Almost every night of my life I had gone to sleep with the sounds of Klaskanine Creek. I wondered if Seaside would have a Klaskanine Creek with Johnny-jump-ups and sour grass on its banks, and grass and moss and alder trees, and swimming holes and trout and crawfish.

Mother said she wasn't sure about a creek and frogs but it had two small rivers and an ocean that was bigger than all of the United States. Once, at the end of World War I when my cousins Bud and Dorothy Banks from Canada were visiting us, we had all gone to Seaside to wade in the ocean. I could see then that it was big but I didn't know it was bigger than the whole United States.

Leaving Klaskanine Creek, we walked up the railroad track past where Uncle Marsh and Aunt Blanche had lived. They now lived in Portland and Aunt Blanche was teaching school. I thought of all the oatmeal and sugar cookies and fresh milk Aunt Blanche had fed me and wished she were there with some now.

The thought of Uncle Marsh and Aunt Blanche reminded Mother of how many close friends had left the camp since the end of the war and during the depression that followed. Some of those who had left moved to other camps; some, like Mr. Peets and Mr. Boyle, tried their hands at farming. It reminded me that outside of Howard Tate, who had now finished grammar school, I was the only youngster of walking age left in the camp.

We walked on up the tracks past the machine shop where Dad worked, past the old familiar office and commissary where

Mr. Bramble and Mrs. Johnson had matched wits so many times. I took a detour through the shop to say hello to Dad and good-by to the other men who worked there. At the cookhouse we said good-by to the Wilsons and Mrs. Wilson gave me a big slab of hot bread just out of the oven with a layer of melting butter spread over it. I knew that no matter how exciting Seaside might be, it could never produce anything to match the Western Cooperage cookhouse with its big wood range and daily output of hot bread, rolls, and pastries.

From the cookhouse we walked up past the wood yard, past the powder house, and on up past the storage tracks that, when the Western Cooperage used to log full blast, were always filled with railroad cars of logs.

Finally we reached the faint little path that led from the railroad tracks to our hideaway spot. Without thinking I turned in there. Mother was close behind.

We knelt at the mossy old log that was our prayer log and altar. Mother had her talk with God first. She didn't say much and sometimes her voice was so low I could hardly hear what she was saying. She asked for guidance and help in setting up our new home in Seaside away from Dad. She asked God to watch over all of us and to help me in adjusting to a new life in a new place.

When my turn came I asked God to take care of our camp and Klaskanine Creek, and the forest, and to keep them there so that when I grew up I could come back.

Mother reached over and took my hand. She squeezed it real hard.

She said it was a real nice prayer, and that God would remember.

Epilogue

There really isn't much more to say.

It is the year 1977 and the old Western Cooperage camp as I knew it is gone. Klaskanine Creek still bubbles and chortles its way to Youngs River and the sea; what used to be the railroad tracks is now a graveled forest road; all of the Johnsons, including Fen and Jake, are dead; Dad and Mother are gone, Uncle Marsh and Aunt Blanche are gone, as are the Robinsons, Jim Irving, the Peetses, O'Hoyts, Lena Boyle, and most of the rest.

Three of my logging camp school teachers are still alive and at intervals we correspond. One, Marguerite Pinnell, who was my second grade teacher and who later married Mr. George Brunner and moved to the Potter and Chester camp, lives in Bakersfield, California. She and her husband eventually went to work for Mr. Hearst at his San Simeon, California, castle. Mr. Brunner died years ago but Mrs. Brunner worked until her retirement a few years ago, cataloguing and bringing order to the Hearst family collection of art and artifacts.

Mr. Foss Cox, the locomotive engineer, is hale and hearty, and well in his eighties. He lives in the small community of Carlton, Oregon. Mrs. Ziak, the little bride that Mother took such a liking to, lives at Knappa, not far from the Columbia

197

River town of Astoria, Oregon. I see her quite often. Emma Holm Splester, a teen-ager who used to baby-sit me when Mother would go off to the woods with Dad to take photographs of logging for the family album, lives a five-minute drive from me in Astoria.

I never did become the civil engineer that Mother hoped for; or the policeman that Dad would have settled for; or the locomotive engineer that I prayed for. Nor did I bring glory to the Churchill name in the academic field. The fact is I failed miserably in college, and ended up leaving school and returning to the camp that had been my home for so many of my growing-up years. The old name Western Cooperage was no more. It was now Tidewater Timber Company and Dad was still working in the shop.

When I left school and returned to the camp to work Mother was broken-hearted; Dad was furious.

"Of all the tomfool dumb things to do," he stormed, marching back and forth across the calk-splintered wood floor of the bunkhouse I had been assigned to share with him.

I tried to explain that it was just something I had to do. I wanted to be like him. And for a time I was. Not as big, not as powerfully built, not as wise in the way of the woods and the expertise of logging. But I wore calk shoes, stagged pants, and a hickory shirt and worked on the rigging.

I worked only a few years in the camps when I began to realize I was seeing the end of an era. The camp was old and looking tired; Dad and Mother were no longer young. The vast ranges of Douglas fir, spruce, hemlock, and cedar that Dad and Uncle Marsh had been so certain would last forever were rapidly disappearing and in some areas were already gone.

The fabulous Kerry Line had hauled its last log. Its ties and steel were gone. The big roundhouse at Camp Neverstill sat empty and alone on its concrete foundation. Tidewater Timber Company was nearing an end, as were Big Creek and scores of others.

Hundreds of locomotives and steam donkey engines had worked themselves out of a job. Trucks and the diesel engine had begun to take over.

The glory, the glamour, the nerve-tingling excitement of a career in the woods were beginning to fade. The concept of tree farming, growing trees as a crop, hadn't yet taken hold, so it was that as the great machines were idled, so were the men who had grown up with them.

Dad was nearing seventy but there was no thought of retirement in his mind.

"What will you do if the camp should close?" I asked him one evening after we had finished supper and were back in the bunkhouse.

"It won't close," he said; "there is still timber." He knew what he said wasn't true, but he had to say it. He and all the other Big Sams in the Oregon woods said it, and kept saying it. Why, it had to be true! A forest that as recently as 1911 (the year I was born) went from horizon to horizon, gone? You had to be crazy as hell. "I seen it, man—big, beautiful, and forever. Goddammit, it can't be gone!"

Well, maybe it wasn't gone, not yet anyhow, but it wouldn't be long until it was.

Dad was spared the agony of those last few years of the big trees. He died in 1941, just two months before his granddaughter was born. Mother lived nine years longer. She appreciated those years because, as she said, they gave her time to see and enjoy her grandchildren. She was living with my wife and me in the irrigated agricultural region of Washington State's Yakima Valley. It was a far cry from the big woods of the Oregon coast.

Dad died while at work in the Tidewater Timber Company's machine shop. He died with the smells of engine oil and timber around him and the sounds of machinery and people he knew to comfort him. He had worked in that shop for nineteen years and, except for that summer's work for Mr. Red Mullins at Little Big Creek, had been on the Western Cooperage and Tide-water Timber Company payroll for thirty-one years.

In 1950, a few months after Mother died, I started a career that had never entered our minds during those talks about college and careers when we lived at the old Western Cooperage camp. I became a newspaper man. The editor who hired me said I "had a feel for writing." If I do, it must have come from Mother. Perhaps it was those hours and hours she spent reading to me, or those long, rainy-day sessions listening with Mrs. Johnson, Fen, and Jake as Mother read Thornton W. Burgess's wonderful bird and animal stories.

Or maybe it was just growing up in a logging camp where God and nature were near and the people around you were generous, thoughtful, and brimming with kindness.

Mother lived to see me work in logging camps, in a gold mine, and for a utility company. She shared the fears of war with my wife, Dorothy, while I was with the Navy in the South Pacific during World War II. She watched me become a variety store manager and even a funeral parlor director. But she didn't live to see me become a newspaper man and a writer. For that I am sorry because Mother admired newspaper people and writers.

She often said that people like Dad and Uncle Marshall could leave their footprints in the sands and soils of time but it would be newspaper people and writers who would keep their memory alive for the generations who would follow.

I don't know, but I suppose that is happening. Mother was usually right and so many of the things she predicted have come to pass.

And so now, I guess, it is my turn. I retired from newspapering in 1974 and returned to this old, old town of Astoria where I was born. My wife and I visit the old camp area often. We find it friendly and peaceful. Some of Mr. T. W. Robinson's house is still there. Parts of the old machine shop where Dad worked and died are there. Our children seem to enjoy visiting the spot and one day, I hope, our grandchildren will visit it now and then.

It was the right time and the right place for a young boy to grow up in.

Now, for me, it is the right time and the right place for a grandfather to age and grow mellow in.